BE WHO YOU WANT TO BE!

# HOW TO TRAIN YOUR BUSINESS BRAIN

THE WORKOUT PROGRAMME FOR YOUR MENTAL MUSCLES

OLIVER THOMPSON

white-card

HOW TO TRAIN YOUR BUSINESS BRAIN
by Oliver Thompson

Published by White-Card Editions, London

ISBN 978-0-9571558-1-7



A catalogue record for this book is available from the British Library.

Editor: Anne Newman
Design: Joerg Hartmannsgruber
Illustrations: Giorgio
Printed in the Northern Ireland by W.G. Baird

[ white-card ]

www.white-card.co.uk

Within your training programme there are six 'Brain Boosters'. Each of these focuses on a core topic of self-improvement and includes a number of cognitive workouts to push your thinking, strengthen your behaviours, make you more mentally agile and improve your personal management.

When attempting to find your Business Brain, mental strength is possibly the most critical ingredient. You will need to think in a more resourceful way than previously, and this is especially true in moments of challenge and adversity. Most successful 'models' attract success because of the positive perceptions they place on the world, eliciting a response that aligns with these perceptions.

Positive psychology embraces areas such as happiness, optimism, mindfulness whilst nurturing helpful behaviours and thinking. In sport psychology, for example, believing you 'can' is clearly a vital strand in a winner's DNA.

Striving to be a brilliant Business Brain isn't easy – otherwise everyone would be massively overachieving in everything that they do. But by utilising the key strategies in this book you can truly improve your thinking and, by extension, your results.

## WHAT IS A BUSINESS BRAIN?

Is it …

… the capacity to think differently, so you can create something remarkable and unique?

… the ability to make money quickly and effectively?

… the power to connect to people with empathy and warmth?

… the ability to generate positive change, even when there are fears and doubts?

… being prepared to take the necessary risks for long-term success?

… the mental resilience to overcome rejection and disappointment without losing hope and focus?

I would suggest that a Business Brain is all of the above and potentially much more.

# WHAT IS IT THAT YOU WANT TO ACHIEVE?

Do you want to become an entrepreneur and start your own business? Are you hoping to design and develop a new product? Are you trying to be more serious about your career and become a high achiever? Perhaps you want to develop a team or just improve your personal impact?

Whatever your goal, this book contains the tools that will help you to achieve your vision and develop your Business Brain. As you read through it and complete the workouts you will become a more resourceful, powerful and fulfilled individual. Think of it as a mental-fitness programme – one that contains all the cognitive exercises for success. Like a personal trainer, it will take you through all the strategies you need to realise your business dreams. All you have to do is be curious, stick with it and take action on the workouts provided.

So let's get those mental muscles kick-started in preparation for your workout, so that you can think differently and develop in new and improved ways. To start, write or draw what you want to achieve in the space opposite – just like if you want to get fitter and healthier, you have to consider where you are now and where you want to be, who you need to be to attain your goal and how you are going to become that person.

**Write or draw what you want to achieve.**

Be creative. Be logical. Be precise. Be clear. Be interesting. Let yourself go.

Now you have decided on what you want, let's make your vision come to life.

BRAIN BOOSTER ONE:

# MINDSET

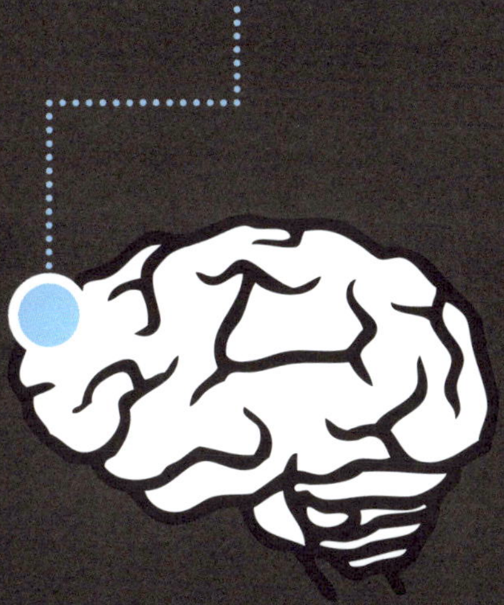

The **PRE-FRONTAL CORTEX** is responsible for planning complex cognitive tasks and appropriate social behaviour. It is thought to be involved in expression of personality.

“SET YOUR SIGHTS HIGH, THE HIGHER THE BETTER. EXPECT THE MOST WONDERFUL THINGS TO HAPPEN, NOT IN THE FUTURE BUT RIGHT NOW. REALISE THAT NOTHING IS TOO GOOD. ALLOW ABSOLUTELY NOTHING TO HAMPER YOU OR HOLD YOU UP IN ANY WAY.

**EILEEN CADDY,**
**FOUNDER OF THE FINDHORN FOUNDATION**

# MISSION POSSIBLE

Most serious companies, including most of the Fortune 500, have a corporate mission statement. A mission statement explains the motivation for being present and answers the questions, 'What are we about and what business are we in?' An enduring statement of purpose, it is designed to provide, among other things, direction and focus to employees and should be the vision that guides you and the people in your business.

In his book *The 7 Habits of Highly Effective People* Stephen Covey explains, as part of his 'second habit', that you must create your own mission: begin with the end in mind and use your personal mission to keep focused and on track.

Just like a business you are your own brand. And to become a successful Business Brain you need to think of yourself as a market leader with a clearly defined mission. Think of this not as arrogance – but more as possessing a clear purpose. You cannot make a difference or be a serious contender if you don't believe in yourself, and to do this you need to clarify your personal mission. Here are some real-life examples for you to ponder:

On a corporate level, Google's mission looks like this:

> " To organise the world's information and make it universally accessible and useful.

On a more personal level, Gandhi's mission was brilliantly delivered in a short list of 'live' statements. You can also bring your mission to life using this style, starting each sentence with 'I shall' or 'I will':

> " Let the first act of every morning be to make the following resolve for the day:
>
> I shall not fear anyone on Earth. I shall fear only God.
> I shall not bear ill will toward anyone.
> I shall not submit to injustice from anyone.
> I shall conquer untruth by truth.
> And in resisting untruth, I shall put up with all suffering.

Entrepreneur Sir Richard Branson's personal mission statement is:

> "To have fun in my journey through life and learn from my mistakes.

... and, he adds:

> "In business, know how to be a good leader and always try to bring out the best in people. It's very simple: listen to them, trust in them, believe in them, respect them, and let them have a go!

Committing to a personal mission offers you the opportunity to establish what's critically important to you. As Steven Covey writes in *First Things First*, it's about 'connecting with your own unique purpose and the profound satisfaction that comes from fulfilling it'.

**1.1** **Create your personal mission here.**
Be specific. Be creative. Be purposeful.

## BEING STEVEN SPIELBERG

Take Spielberg with the multitude of visionary concepts he's created, from *Duel* and *Jaws* to *Schindler's List* and *Minority Report*. Each requires a strong visual focus to achieve stunning, multi-sensory experiences including storyboards, characterisation and emotional hooks.

But what about *your* story, *your* character, *your* team? Becoming a winner means you have to create and visualise a version of your story that means business. Consider the following questions:

- How will my screenplay look? What elements do I see?
- How long is the story? What are the timescales?
- What are the key moments in the story? What challenges does our hero face?
- Who else plays a major part in the story? Who are friends and who are enemies?
- If I were to break the screenplay into separate parts or scenes, what would they be?
- What resources does the lead role have to draw on – mental, physical, monetary, family, personal networks, gadgets, etc.?

Most people who develop into winners don't embark on their championship run saying, 'I hope someday to turn into a champion'. They think about that goal each and every day, and do everything in their power to make certain it is realised. They live it, they breathe it, they obsess over it.

**1.2** **So, with this in mind, create your screenplay below.**

Draw out the core scenes here:

Who will help my hero achieve their mission?

How long is the screenplay? What time frames make it up?

How can I market the screenplay to make people enjoy it (the USPs)?

# YOUR SUPER SELF

Business Brains who achieve greatness possess many qualities, one of which is an unshakeable self-belief. But how is this attained, especially when there are so many challenges and obstacles littered along the way?

A phrase often used in sport psychology is 'What happens out there is a direct consequence of what happens in there' and it is so relevant in the context of successful thinking. In simple terms, it means that your actual performance is often the result of what's happening mentally or, more specifically, those movies and soundtracks playing inside your head.

A powerful exercise is to visualise the winning you – the version of yourself that has been resourceful and already achieved the desired outcome: the SUPER YOU. It may sound simplistic, but visualising the *best version of you* is a technique used by the most successful individuals. Winners win because they have a specific way of thinking, they set definite goals and they are committed to their purpose. They place all of their energy, willpower and effort into achieving their ambitions, and setbacks and losses do not weaken their desire – they make it burn stronger.

So expand your *self*. Have some fun and create your 'Super-Self' identity.

## 1.3 What would the Super Self look like?

How would they behave, dress and act?

How would they feel and think?

How would they be described by others?

# SUPER-SELF-TALK

Winning Business Brains commonly exhibit remarkable displays of resilience. Hoping and wishing are really just statements of good intent, but rarely bring achievement. With a solid state of mind, however, and a well thought-out success strategy backed up with endurance, persistence and a 'won't-settle-for-failure' mindset, you will be victorious.

Success can be a lonely business. It can also be rather hard work and calls for a capacity to deal with many challenging individuals and dismissive attitudes, all of which can lead to negative self-talk. This can be disempowering, especially if your own commentary includes phrases like:

I am not certain …

If only I didn't …

I wish I could …

I don't know how …

I can't believe that this …

Why doesn't it …

But I …

Anyone who has achieved a level of success has faced adversity and obstacles at some point: no support, lack of funding, poor resources, mental or physical pain and fatigue, poor working conditions, strong opponents to their ideals. The only way to succeed in the face of these difficulties is to have powerful self-belief, drive, passion, focus and self-worth. And positive self-talk is one tool that is vital in making things happen.

The following are three key steps to changing your Self, so that it works for you rather than against you.

**Step 1** Examine your identity and the internal language you use

Self-talk is often so habitual that people are unaware that it is going on at all. If you are going to change your self-talk, you need to be aware of these thoughts as they happen. Take some time to notice the things you say to yourself during your day.

**1.4a** **Write them below:**

**Step 2** **Evaluate the perceptions of your current identity**

Who are you? Are your perceptions mainly negative or positive? If they are negative, ask yourself these questions:

- What evidence is there to support this thought?
- What evidence is there against it?
- Is this the way I would talk to a friend who was in my position?
- What are the positive ways of viewing this situation?
- Am I really keeping things in perspective?
- Even if there is some validity to this thought, how useful is it spending my energy thinking about it?

**Answer the above questions here:** 1.4b

**Step 3** Use your Super Self

If you decide that your self-talk is unhelpful or wrong, replace the negative thoughts with your Super Self. Imagine yourself leading with confidence, winning that deal or making the perfect speech. Invest just five minutes after waking up on running through what today will look like in your head, creating a cognitive association that connects you to your Super Self. Be the lead in the film of your life – because if you don't believe in yourself, how do you expect anything to work for you?

**1.4c** **Write or draw what you want today to look like as your Super Self.**

## ROLE MODEL

Changing self-talk requires some time and practice, since our ways of thinking tend to be quite ingrained, and you will probably need to keep working on these steps for some time before it becomes second nature.

To support your resourceful new Super Self, commit to exploring the biographies of successful people in business. Notice their attitudes in trying to win and use this information to educate youself.

What if you spent time with a successful person? Let's say an Oprah Winfrey, Steve Jobs, Anita Roddick or Paul Smith. Ask yourself:

- What can I learn from their experiences?
- How might that help me?
- What obstacles did they face and how can I relate them to my experience?
- How would thinking like them be helpful?
- How would they behave in my situation?
- How much more quickly could I achieve success if I used their approach?
- If I did xyz how much would my performance improve?

**Using two or three successful people as your models – people you admire or who have achieved a similar mission to yours – answer the questions above. What has this taught you?** 1.5

The inventors and aviation pioneers ORVILLE & WILBUR WRIGHT battled depression and family illness before starting the bicycle shop that would lead them to experimenting with flight. After numerous attempts at creating flying machines, several years of hard work and countless failed prototypes, the brothers finally created a plane that could get airborne and stay there.

# FALLING IS GOOD

Business Brains know that our mental landscape and what we believe can limit our effectiveness, whether as communicators, leaders or, equally, as parents, coaches or teachers. These limiting 'maps', if you like, may have been created from experiences we've had.

Some maps don't quite work out how you would hope they will. They were painful or embarrassing so they shape how you anticipate things will be from now on.

Success doesn't often happen immediately. In fact most Business Brains know that everyone makes mistakes and experiences setbacks. But you have a choice. You can *a)* think like an unresourceful adult – give up and decide that you are now incapable or *b)* think like a baby learning to walk – be free from negative mapped experiences and persist until you succeed. Babies treat each effort as a learning experience. To achieve their success winners also explore their results, they try to understand what they have learnt and apply it to every new attempt. These experiences are simply feedback and therefore if treated as such have immense benefits.

**What have you failed at but persisted with so you eventually achieved what you set out to do?** **1.6a**

Name three things you did specifically to make this happen?

1)

2)

3)

**1.6b** **Let's dig deeper shall we? It's always a good idea to connect your thinking to your desired vision. Produce a simple SWOT analysis of you relating to your outcome:**

| | | | |
|---|---|---|---|
| **S** | **Strengths**<br>What are you good at? | **W** | **Weaknesses**<br>What are you not so good at? |
| **O** | **Opportunities**<br>What choices can you create to help you? | **T** | **Threats**<br>What's threatening your chances of success? |

**1.6c** **What feedback have you got from this exercise? How can you use it to take action and strengthen your chances of achieving your outcome?**

# CHOOSING CHOICE

As mentioned earlier, we always have a choice. It is just that sometimes our choices can be perceived as painful, ludicrous or just too plain risky. But don't ignore them because they are still messages that can direct your attention. They may be saying: 'If you choose this path, then this outcome may become a possibility, so make sure you focus on something else more constructive.'

At the other extreme, some choices may seem too easy or obvious! But explore them too. The more options you create, the more opportunities arise, and new discoveries with them. Winners think about the 'What if I ...?' and 'How would that serve me?'

The problem with choice is that it is often easier to fail at something than to succeed. Yep ... think about it. If you wanted to start your own business, for example, you could easily think of many reasons why it would be a bad idea. Why it would fail. And why you wouldn't be good enough to make it a success.

**Not enough capital** **No experience** **Too much to risk**

**Lack of skills** **The competition are better placed**

To focus on the few core choices that would help make it a possibility becomes much trickier as they are outgunned by the doubtful alternatives.

But to be a Business Brain you need to understand that weighing up choice really is a powerful route to success. It helps you to evaluate your purpose and set a path towards making things happen. Create choices that are in line with your Super Self, your mission and your desired outcomes. Creating choice can help you minimise risk and maximise focus, understand the challenges before they appear and stimulate new and more powerful options as you recognise them materialising.

**1.7a** **Think about your choices – which are limited and could prevent a successful outcome?**

**1.7b** **Now, using your Super Self – what new choices could you make to help generate a successful outcome?**

You see, already you are creating more effective choices through more empowering questions.

BRAIN BOOSTER TWO:

# RELATIONSHIPS

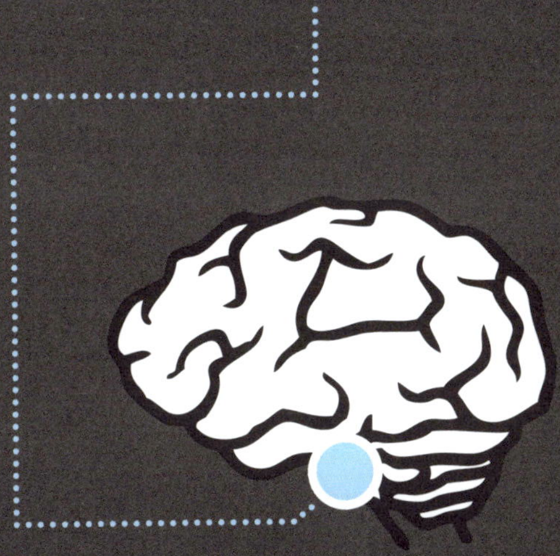

The **HYPOTHALAMUS** controls body temperature, hunger, thirst and your sleep-wake cycle – unconscious physical reactions that greatly influence attachment behaviour.

"FLATTER ME, AND I MAY NOT BELIEVE YOU. CRITICISE ME, AND I MAY NOT LIKE YOU. IGNORE ME, AND I MAY NOT FORGIVE YOU. ENCOURAGE ME, AND I WILL NOT FORGET YOU. LOVE ME AND I MAY BE FORCED TO LOVE YOU.

**WILLIAM ARTHUR WARD,**
**AMERICAN AUTHOR**

**The key to successful interactions with people** – relationships, if you like – can be simply described with the following metaphor.

You can choose to look at a situation using a mirror or a window. If you always use a mirror you will see everything relating back to you. You will be using your own filters: your needs, your values, your beliefs, your emotions. If you like what you see, you will probably have constructive responses. But if you don't, then your responses may well be destructive, based on the event not making sense to the ego within you – your reflected self.

If, on the other hand, you look at the situation through a window, you will be exploring an external view. You will be examining what's actually going on outside in the world around you and viewing experiences as others may see them. You will see others and their environment. You will learn because it's not always as you thought or want. People often only respond in line with their past experiences and quite often need us to help them see the same thing in a number of different, resourceful ways. However, if this is the only way you view things, then you may be placing other people's needs before your own and therefore not allowing yourself to focus on the drivers that your inner self requires.

Mirrors are great if you need to re-evaluate your own performance and to find inner focus and strength in tough times. Think about using mirrors to maximise your time – to help you see what you need to do in the time allocated and stick to it by saying 'No' to time thieves and distractions.

Windows are often used by Business Brains in leadership positions. They help you to see how others need motivating and to share successes. Windows are equally strong when networking because they help you to listen, engage and share ideas and future actions.

When it comes to relationships, try removing the mirror and opening a window. It may just help you see things more clearly.

# HEART AND HEAD

Emotional intelligence or EQ (emotional quotient) is a behavioural model, famously explored in Daniel Goleman's 1995 book *Emotional Intelligence*. As the need for personal engagement within organisations has grown, EQ has become more and more widely acknowledged. Understanding EQ supports the leadership-led mind and the increasing need to develop talent because it provides a new way to understand and evaluate people's behaviour, communication styles, attitudes, interpersonal skills and potential. As such, EQ plays an important part in recruitment and selection, coaching strategies, staff development, PR, customer relations, pitching, selling and leading.

Emotional intelligence also has strong links with strategies around connection, empathy and spirituality: bringing compassion and mindfulness to work. The EQ concept argues that IQ (intelligence quotient), or conventional intelligence, is too narrow – that there are wider areas of intelligence that dictate and enable how successful we are. We've all met people who are academically brilliant and yet are socially and interpersonally inept. And we know that success does not automatically follow a high IQ rating.

Business Brains with high EQ know they can implement strategies while also motivating individual team members in a uniquely appropriate way. And when selling they can influence people without damaging motives while creating a well-organised project plan.

Emotional intelligence is built on the foundations of two specific levels – interpersonal and intrapersonal:

Interpersonal (windows) Knowledge and Information vs Wisdom and Awareness. You may read books on law, quantum physics and computer mechanics, but this doesn't mean that you necessarily get on well with other people, can empathise with and understand them or communicate with them effectively.

Intrapersonal (mirrors) Connecting with other people isn't the same as being able to understand your own emotional inner self. Intrapersonal intelligence is the ability to manage yourself and become more self-aware – to know who you are and what makes you tick.

Now, think about someone you need to engage with successfully. Perhaps they can support your business or team? Maybe they are difficult to deal with and you need to find a way to gain a mutual understanding? Try using EQ here.

2.1

**Think of a client or colleague who is important to reaching your goal. Ask yourself the following questions:**

How do I see them and what do I notice about them?

How might my response not be helping?

What could I do differently to create better synergy?

# THE EQ ASPIRIN

Time is often wasted on unresolved conflict with negative emotional responses serving little or no purpose in terms of the core outcomes of your business or goals. However, high-EQ thinkers resolve conflict quickly and effectively and are therefore able to deliver high performance.

Here are some areas where EQ can really make a difference:

**Untapped potential.** People use approximately 30 per cent of their potential at work, mainly because they don't have a leader or mentor to encourage them or to unlock hidden skills. EQ Business Brains develop their teams and provide opportunities for individuals to express themselves more effectively.

**Lost customers and lower referral rates.** To create an advocate for your business means taking an existing customer and generating service built around trust, respect, quality and appreciation – all EQ-led attributes.

**Cost of stress-related illnesses.** Modern life is now more and more technology-reliant. However, health is based around the mind-body connection. So when it comes to wellbeing you can forget iPads and tablets – how you think and feel about the world often dictates how you respond to situations and being able to use EQ thinking will make you more mentally resilient and mindful.

**Unresourceful thinking.** While limited and restrictive mindsets can create a sense of safety, security and comfort, if you truly want to make a difference then you should never stop learning. The world evolves and you need to evolve with it to become truly successful. EQ Business Brains know that their reality is simply a reflection of how they have filtered their experience and the world around them, and this makes them more aware and responsive in their behaviour.

**Coaching and influencing.** EQ Business Brains understand the need to 'get people on board' with their ideas and concepts. The ability to shape people's thinking towards your ideas is a true benefit in business.

# EQ: THE SIX DOMAINS

EQ is an extremely powerful concept. It embodies the most accessible, positive and useful elements of modern psychology, and so can be helpful in virtually every aspect of personal and interpersonal relations. EQ is beneficial for self-development, as well as for businesses and organisations.

| | |
|---|---|
| Knowing and managing your own emotions | Knowing how to generate solid outcomes |
| Becoming agile and flexible in your thinking | Understanding rapport and empathy |
| Becoming more self-aware | Being the best version of you |

2.2

**How and where can you practise all of these attributes to support yourself on your mission? List six ways below.**

1.

2.

3.

4.

5.

6.

# WHAT'S YOUR POSITIVE INTENTION?

Simply put, at some level all behaviour has a positive purpose.

The positive purpose supporting certain aggressive behaviour, for example, may be protection. The positive intention behind intimidation can often be driven by a need for controlling someone or perceived power over others. The positive purpose behind fear is often safety. The positive purpose behind anger can be to maintain boundaries. Hate may have the positive purpose for motivating a person to take action. The positive intentions behind something like resistance to change could encompass a range of issues including the desire to acknowledge, honour or respect the past, a need to protect oneself by staying with the familiar and an attempt to hold on to the positive things one has had in the past.

Sometimes a particular challenging behaviour or symptom may even serve multiple positive intentions. An example may be someone who rarely sees things through to the end. They may start something because it is interesting and stimulating. They may then get other people involved because they enjoy the attention and the recognition of being thought of as popular. They may then decide not to complete the thing that got them so excited initially because a new distraction feeds the original feeling of stimulation they have since lost. They may not want the growing pressure of expectation, so they down tools to avoid this. Or they may simply feel that their idea is proving too time-consuming, so they start doing the stuff they enjoy more and fulfils their real values.

The best Business Brains understand how to use positive intention to their advantage. They know the three things to consider within this context:

**People are more than just their behaviour.** People's actions are based on their own, often unconscious, positive intention rather than being designed to damage you or your goals. By knowing this you can help others develop by broadening their views rather than attacking their actions.

**Judgement can be suspended.** Because you now have a great awareness of why people perhaps behave in perceived odd and damaging ways you can suspend negative judgement and work on education rather than ridicule or frustration.

**Focused positive intention.** You need to invest time understanding what motivates you and what motivates those around you. In order to maximise everyone's positive intentions, learn that we are all driven towards our motivators and will act in ways that support or reinforce them.

2.3

**Now that you understand positive intention, why not think of some of your own potentially challenging behaviours that may not support your mission.**

Once you've identified these, seek the potential positive intention for each of them, then think about how you could move away from these behaviours and find more resourceful alternatives – or even change the intention behind them to something that is more supportive:

| Behaviour | Positive intention | Alternative behaviour/ intention |
|---|---|---|
| | | |

# EXCUSES DRIVE YOU NOWHERE

It's easy for you, but difficult for me because ...

I am too busy.

I seriously can't afford the time and effort to do that.

I've tried, but I couldn't because ...

We've all made these types of comments to ourselves and others while defending why we aren't doing the things we say we want to do. But why? Well, because more often than not it's easier to make excuses than to actually get up and push ourselves to achieve the success we are looking for. Success isn't easy, but it can be simple – just like failure.

Imagine trying to lose weight. The simplest formula is to reduce your calorie intake and exercise more, so you can burn off any excess. But that means accepting that you need to change, which can be scary. It may mean you have to open yourself up to criticism or pressure, which could be upsetting; or it may mean having to restrict yourself to less familiar choices, and this can create undesirable discomfort initially.

All of these responses are built around fear – probably human nature's biggest driver. Fear means we get to sit back and feel perversely smug about how we have it harder than other people. We get to play the victim because 'they' have no idea how tough it is. We develop a passive attitude whenever we talk about the changes we would make and the desires we would pursue 'if only' our situation were different.

Often, however, it's not our problems that are the issue; it's actually how we think about them that generates our limitations.

Let's take money. Money is not a problem, but if we value supporting others through kindness and associate wealth with greed and status then quite often we can negate positive financial gains by acting in reflection of these beliefs. We may say 'I don't deserve this because many other people are much worse off than me.' We may reject accepting financial kindness because we feel it lacks any real emotional meaning. We may live below our earning potential because being financially secure almost compromises the social position we're currently comfortable living with.

Let's look again. Being empathetic can often be seen by many as a sign of weakness. We could view empathy through a lens of actions associated with 'pink, fluffy and oversensitive'. You may say that 'Understanding others doesn't make you a success. You need to be selfish to win'. This is simply devaluing a strong behavioural trait through which we can interact with others more effectively and create winning relationships.

**Write down one trait or talent that you know would support your progress even though you often create an excuse that negates its power:**

2.4

So, what's the excuse you use?

# RESOURCEFUL NOT FORCEFUL

Ultimately, you can never control how other people think, but you can increase your awareness of their patterns of thought by monitoring their emotions and behaviours. If someone is displaying negative emotions or unresourceful performance behaviours, then the root cause is their internal dialogue at that specific moment in time.

There will be a temptation for you to analyse 'what they don't want', but there is no need as you will be focusing your attention in the wrong direction. As long as appropriate time has been invested in creating a detailed picture of the 'mission' or 'what we want to achieve' then the path to success will be to refocus them on the vision of winning performance and the vital contribution that they can deliver.

A number of factors may be at play when it comes to weakened thinking:

Fear of success: How will I be perceived by my friends? What will change if I succeed?

Feelings of worthlessness: I'm not good enough.

Fear of failure: What if I get it wrong?

Lack of confidence in ability: What if I am incapable of achieving what is being asked?

Lack of inspiration: I just don't care.

Fear of judgement: How will others see me?

Lack of engagement: Do I really have to?

It is inevitable that you will experience one or more of the above doubts at some point – even Usain Bolt can have a bad day. But the mark of a true winner is determined by their resilience and commitment to maintain resourceful thinking, regardless of the situation around them – to create an environment that supports and nurtures strong, resourceful thinking among friends, colleagues, clients and employees in the bad times as well as the good.

Does the current environment in your organisation enhance resourceful thinking in your people?

| Resourceful Business Brain | Unresourceful Business Brain |
|---|---|
| Seeks solutions in times of pressure | Adds to the pressure through forcing opinion |
| Knows that 'If I can do it so can you' | Thinks that they are the only one capable |
| Matches roles to capabilities | Treats people like machines |
| Trusts and appreciates each individual | Openly criticises performance |
| Nurtures the talent in their teams | Struggles to delegate |
| Recognises each success | Recognises each failure |
| Accepts failures and builds solutions | Always apportions blame |
| Inspires creativity and new ideas | Directs how tasks must be accomplished |
| Values the individual perspective of each team member | Manages everyone in a similar fashion |
| Communicates openly and readily | Communicates only on a 'need-to-know' basis |
| Encourages growth and development of new skills | Delivers minimal training |

# WHY DO YOU EXIST, FOLKS?

An undefined brand is unmarketable. Hence Steve Jobs shared the two questions Apple started with to bring the company back from the brink of collapse:

Who is Apple and what does Apple stand for? And where do we fit in this world?

Steve Jobs knew the difference between the whats and whys. That Apple makes products for people to get their jobs done more effectively only highlights what Apple does. But here's Apple's 'why' according to Jobs: 'Apple believes that people with passion can change the world for the better. And those people that are crazy enough to think that they can, are the ones who actually do.' Because of this many people have become advocates and possess an unshakable loyalty to Apple's brand.

What do you believe your product or service truly achieves? The WHY.

Business brains understand that we need to pitch to the emotional or the reptilian part of our Brains. This is the place where we truly care. This helps us to engage with our own personal beliefs and values and if your product or service resonates with these thoughts we will sit up and listen.

The 'what you do' is the boring bit. It is a only a factual representation of your product or service, and undoubtedly you will have competitors offering the same or similar. It does not help you to differentiate yourself, it is uninspiring and certainly doesn't instigate any action.

The 'how you do things' is a little more interesting but you can't lead in with that as this is the 'technical or process based element'. Again, if it's not interesting why would they listen?

Rather than pitch 'what you do' , 'how you do it' and then 'what it will mean', go and switch the order.

Start with the WHY – this is where we create emotional engagement. Next discuss the 'how it can be done' – your method. And finally the 'what you do' – your solution.

**2.5a** **What does your product or service truly stand for?**
The EMOTION or VALUE

**2.5b** **Next, how do you bring this to life?**
The METHOD of making this happen

**2.5c** **Finally, what you do?**
The actual SOLUTION

Example: this book is for people who believe that they have the potential to achieve something special. The people who don't want to settle and want to maximise their talents. That's *why* it's of value.

It allows you to explore your ideas, identity and personal brand, so you can shape yourself more effectively to be who and where you want to be. That's *how* it brings this to life.

The book works because it's proactive. Not only does it talk about models and concepts of thinking and behaviour, but it helps you to work these ideas out for yourself. That's *what* it does.

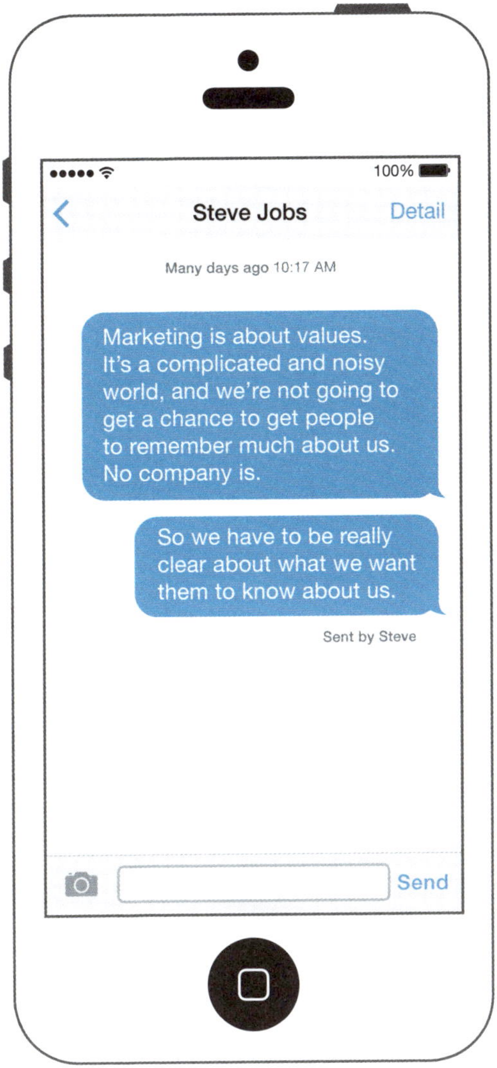
100%
Steve Jobs
Detail
Many days ago 10:17 AM
Marketing is about values. It's a complicated and noisy world, and we're not going to get a chance to get people to remember much about us. No company is.
So we have to be really clear about what we want them to know about us.
Sent by Steve
Send

# YOUR NETWORK = YOUR NET WORTH

Ask any successful Business Brain and they will tell you that networking and developing strong relationships is one of the key criteria for success. Your personal network is your net worth. Research shows that the best jobs are never advertised and 85 per cent of all jobs are found through networking. Ignore developing your networking skills at your peril.

Here are some helpful considerations to support your ability to network:

- Every connection must have a win–win in mind: make the interaction mutually beneficial.
- Learn to enjoy meeting new people and make it one of the joys of your working life.
- Be curious. Never stop listening to the people you network with as you may miss something.
- If going to networking groups never do so with the intention of simply handing out business cards to as many people as possible. Research the group first and perhaps target three or four other interesting and relevant networkers. Then, if it's worthwhile, arrange to meet them properly for a coffee to talk more.

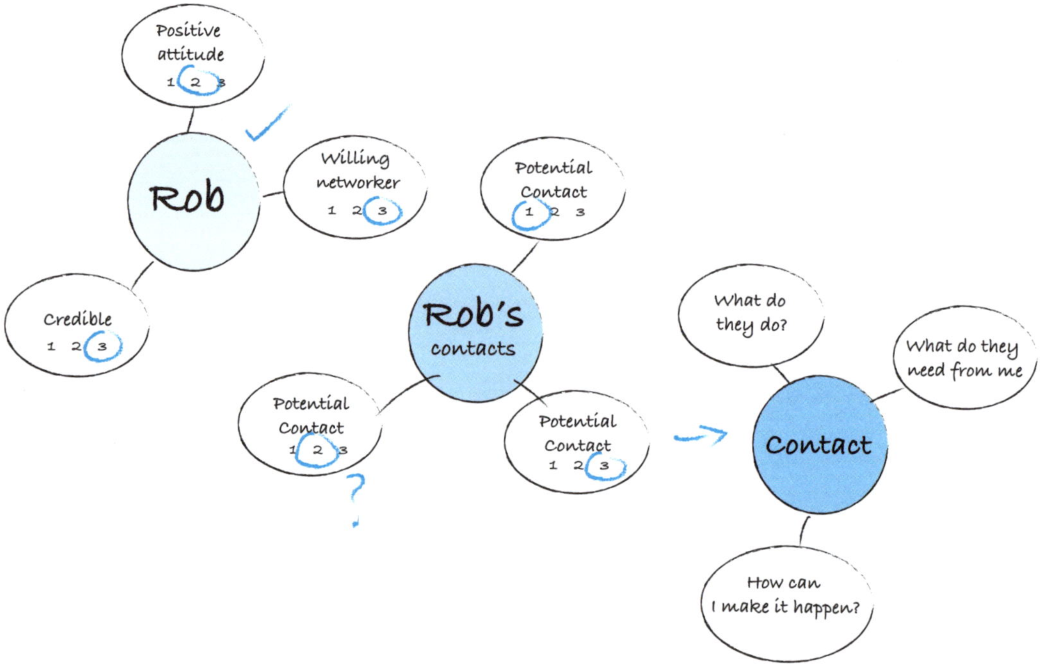

**Below is a really powerful method for creating opportunities from your personal network – this exercise will open doors and help you fulfil your mission:**

2.6

1 **Names:** draw a circle in the centre of a blank sheet of A4 paper and in it write the name of a member of your family who is employed.

2 **Capability:** draw three more circles connected to that central one and label them:
Circle 1: Positive attitude (would they be open to an approach by you to ask for their help?)
Circle 2: Willing networker (are they good at networking and do they understand its value?)
Circle 3: Credible (are they well thought of in both their aptitude and approach to business?)

3 **Act:** score each of these elements on a scale of 1–3, where 1 = low, 2 = moderate and 3 = high. If they are a 1 on any of these scales, it may be tricky to receive their networking support. As an example, Rob scores 2 for positive attitude, 3 for willing networker and 3 for credible. This evaluation means Rob could be a good door opener.

4 **Rank:** next, draw three circles to represent three contacts the person in the central circle has and rank them from 1 to 3 in terms of their relevance to you. Then dismiss any level 1 contacts.

5 **Value:** now take each relevant contact and ask yourself:
1) What do they do?
2) What do they need from me?
3) How can I make this happen?
This will help you to make your communication relevant and, of course, of value to both parties.

6 **Don't stop:** keep the flow going and expand your network until you feel it's exhausted. Think of more friends, family members, associates, social contacts, suppliers and existing clients.

**Now get in touch with them!**

BRAIN BOOSTER THREE:

# PERCEPTION

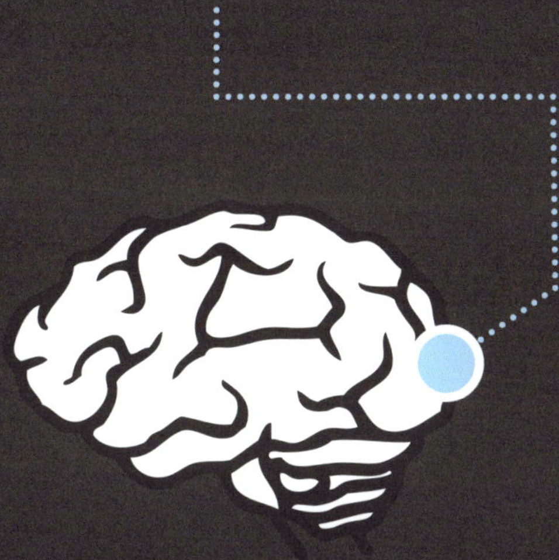

The **OCCIPITAL LOBE** receives and interprets visual input.

“WHAT YOU SEE AND WHAT YOU HEAR DEPENDS A GREAT DEAL ON WHERE YOU ARE STANDING.
IT ALSO DEPENDS ON WHAT SORT OF PERSON YOU ARE.

**C. S. LEWIS,**
**NOVELIST AND POET**

**Our success is largely dependent on how we perceive ourselves** and the world around us. How we view everything within us and around us affects our attitudes to life:

The optimistic Business Brain will generate success because they possess self-belief.

The curious Business Brain will explore life and create solutions and ideas, regardless of the odds.

The logical Business Brain will evaluate all options available and take calculated risks.

The emotionally intelligent Business Brain will find support and love the thrill of creating success for themselves and others.

The resourceful Business Brain will enjoy the challenges life throws at them and will make the most of every opportunity.

The pessimistic Business Brain will find challenges difficult and struggle to view life as anything other than painful.

All of the above approaches are simply created from perceptions we generate from our experiences. Imagine if you could achieve your purpose in life. How would you need to see things?

# IF WHAT YOU'RE DOING ISN'T WORKING, DO SOMETHING DIFFERENT

Put simply: modify your behaviour. Business Brains know it's better to change tactics than to continue along the path of failure. You can increase your flexibility by freeing yourself from limiting beliefs. You know you are limited by your beliefs when you use expressions such as 'I have to', 'I should', 'I can't', or 'I must never'. The use of these expressions implies you also act under compulsion – your limiting beliefs restrict the choice of options available to you. Each time such an expression comes to your mind, stop and think about what would happen if you didn't 'have to'. Usually, nothing much would actually happen, but you would gain a lot more freedom to act in the way you want.

You can be flexible by adopting a different perspective. When you encounter seemingly insurmountable problems, try to see them from another person's point of view. Ask yourself, 'What would X do in my position to successfully deal with it?' This will go a long way towards helping you arrive at a solution.

Try out as many perspectives as you can to help increase your flexibility.

3.1

**Taking a limiting viewpoint you hold or perhaps a past situation that has never really helped you move forward, consider how someone else would view it if they had no emotional connection? What would they say and what advice would they give?**

**Next, how would a successful sports star treat the situation?**
Say, a Chris Hoy or a Jessica Ennis.

**And how would a successful business person view it and what would they do?**
Elle Macpherson or Donald Trump.

# THE ART OF FRAMING

If you have ever visited a gallery or purchased a work of art, you will probably know that a frame has almost as much impact on how you view a painting as the painting itself. Similarly, if you think about how you view a specific challenge, often it can simply be a part of your thinking that's the problem and not the situation itself. Perhaps if you improved your thinking, you might also improve the situation or outcome.

So, the way we look at a problem and the frame we give it, can make it easier or harder to solve. We use frames of thinking to provide a context, focus or guidance for our thoughts and actions. And different cognitive frames have different uses. They might keep us on track, for example, lend a focus for our activities, ensure we are congruent with our goals, supply evaluation on our progress, help us to explore new possibilities or support a common understanding.

Framing helps us to develop the ability to step out of an experience and take a second position, therefore allowing us to understand differing perspectives and learn from them. When we activate another frame, we reframe our position, perspective and, consequently, the meaning we infer. We begin to explore our normal experiences with new views, so we can see things in different ways, hear opinions more clearly, feel new types of emotions and begin to speak and act in more original ways.

### Try basic reframing of the event

To start you off, think about a negative event in your life. Perhaps a meeting wasn't received well, an important relationship broke down or you started a project that simply never came to fruition. Now, think about what you could have possibly gained from this in terms of learning, acting or thinking.

3.2

**Take a negative situation in your life and ask yourself:**
Even though it was painful, what can I take from this experience?
Although it didn't work at the time, what did I learn and how can this help me next time?
It wasn't easy, but why did it happen to me and what could the positive intention be?

# YOU'VE BEEN FRAMED

Now we know how helpful framing our thoughts can be, let's go a little deeper. It's all too easy to be negative and to create something like the Blame Frame:

Who can I blame?

What did they do wrong?

Why didn't they do what I asked?

Outcome-framed questions, on the other hand, are resourceful. They keep your attention on the goal and on what needs to happen for it to be realised. Here are some examples of more positive questions you might ask yourself:

Where am I now (my present situation A)?

Where do I want to be (my desired outcome B)?

What resources do I need to move from A to B?

What is my plan of action to narrow the gap between A and B?

What will I experience once B is achieved?

Let's try another example – The Possibility Frame. Set out your situation by framing your thoughts around what you 'can do', rather than what you 'cannot do' or 'have to do'. Focus on potential. Look at new options and opportunities:

What is possible?

What would have to happen for this to be possible?

How could I make this possible?

What isn't possible?

Words or phrases often used in the context of possibility include: could / options / choice / feasible / make / ideas / interesting / create / if we can / may.

**Try to create some more possibility-framed questions.**

3.3

Other frames you could use include:

Cause and effect: this frame allows you to understand and focus on the relationship between what you are doing and the results you are getting.

As if: ask yourself what would happen if you acted and behaved as if you had already achieved the outcomes? What would you experience if you were acting as the best role model you can find in this area? This focuses your attention on becoming a more resourceful version of yourself to give yourself a better chance of success.

Curious: this removes assumptions. As we know, assumptions limit our thinking, but if you are interested or curious, that allows you to open your mind and explore. Start your questions with 'I'm interested to know ... ' or 'That's fascinating, how have you ... '

Feedback: rather than wallow in an unsuccessful attempt at something, try adding feedback to what happened. What did you learn? If you did it again, how would you approach things differently? Who do you know could help you next time?

# LIFE THROUGH A LENS

When you have a disagreement with someone or you just don't understand why they have done something, put on a different pair of glasses and look at the world, and yourself, from their point of view. Aim to adopt their map of the situation, rather than just thinking 'What would I do in that situation?' Start from a position which seems to make sense to them and is compatible with their values and beliefs, and build bridges to where you want them to get to. You will also get better-quality information if you match their words, tone and physiology – talk as they talk, stand as they stand, breathe as they breathe and so on.

To avoid the cognitive error of 'mind-reading', remember that the intuition you get from this is just a guess about what the other person is thinking and feeling. Business Brains always check out their intuition against what the person actually does.

When trying to achieve, explore the boundaries of your own map. Where are the limits of your map? What do you feel you can't do, or you don't deserve? The areas in your life that are not going as well as you would like may indicate that your map could do with some tweaks.

Where you have a belief that is not serving you, for example, 'I really dislike having to network', then actively look for examples where that belief does not hold true.

Where you tend to make sweeping generalisations, for example, 'I've always struggled with being too detailed', then actively look for counter-examples.

When you think you can't do something that you would like to do, ask yourself, 'What would happen if I did?'

**3.4** **Think of a relevant situation in your past. Write it down.**

J. K. ROWLING may be incredibly wealthy and successful today, however before she published her first Harry Potter novel she was down on her luck. Depressed, divorced and trying to raise a child on her own while attending school and writing, she went, in only five years, from depending on benefits to survive to being one of the richest women in the world. She did this through her focus, hard work and determination.

# LANDSCAPING YOUR BRAIN

Your mental landscape and what you believe can limit your effectiveness as a Business Brain, communicator and leader or, equally, as a parent, coach, teacher or sports player. So now let's find some ways to change limiting maps. Some of these methods involve stepping back from your existing map and viewing it from a wider perspective (this is very useful if you have a conversation with someone who doesn't share exactly the same belief system as you), while others are about examining the assumptions underpinning the landscape in more detail and comparing it to the reality of your experience.

Start by picking a limiting mental map that you may possess. It could relate to a relationship that you want to improve, a personal view that is not getting you the results you want or perhaps you feel is limiting your personal impact.

3.5 **Write it here:**

**Next, ask yourself some questions:**

Why is it restrictive and unresourceful?

How can you view it differently? Explore your mental landscape.

If you were to view and experience a more resourceful map what would need to change?

What results would occur that perhaps you are not currently experiencing?

Once you can appreciate the perspectives and views reached by others, only then can you truly understand and open up new opportunities for relationships and outcomes. Beliefs are extremely strong and far reaching for many people. They can be empowering or sometimes, sadly, disempowering; they can stimulate positive action or generate restrictive thinking.

Limiting landscapes, maps and beliefs can cause:

- poor states and ways of feeling (such as low self-esteem)
- fears and restrictions (fears of being alone)
- passive actions (apathy)
- a lack of awareness in various contexts (ignorance)
- negative behaviours (depression).

Unlimited maps can generate:

- resourceful states (such as confidence)
- powerful choices (e.g. to leave a bad relationship)
- active actions (immediacy)
- heightened awareness in various contexts (flexibility)
- positive behaviours (assertiveness).

# CHANGING THE LANDSCAPE

So, we know we often need to alter a limiting view and see the landscape more clearly with a wider-reaching perspective of everything (as in the case of a conversation with someone who doesn't share exactly the same belief system as you), while others are about examining the assumptions underpinning the thought or belief in more detail and comparing it to the reality of your experience.

3.6a **Pick a limited landscape that you may possess and write it here:**

Why is it restrictive and unresourceful?

Now try the 'stepping back' technique. Specifically, it's about stepping back from being immersed in the moment and looking at the future consequences of continuing to hold that unresourceful mapped belief. The question to ask yourself is, 'If I go on believing this, what will be the consequences?'

**You can go into more detail by looking at specific areas:**

3.6b

What will be the consequences for me today?
What will be the consequences for the mission?
What will be the consequences for my team and the people supporting me?

When we become convinced that something needs to change, our minds automatically become more resourceful and start looking round for ways to change it. This is useful when it leads to you finding better methods and ideas, but not so useful if it leads to unproductive worry. So you need something that turns your mind's attention to where it is most likely to find the change you need – such as these questions:

**How does it serve me?**

↓

**What do I need to believe/value instead?**

↓

**What steps do I need to take?**

↓

**What would be the new outcome?**

While looking at things in this way won't necessarily change the limiting belief by itself, what it will do is make you more motivated to do something about it.

BRAIN BOOSTER FOUR:

# LANGUAGE

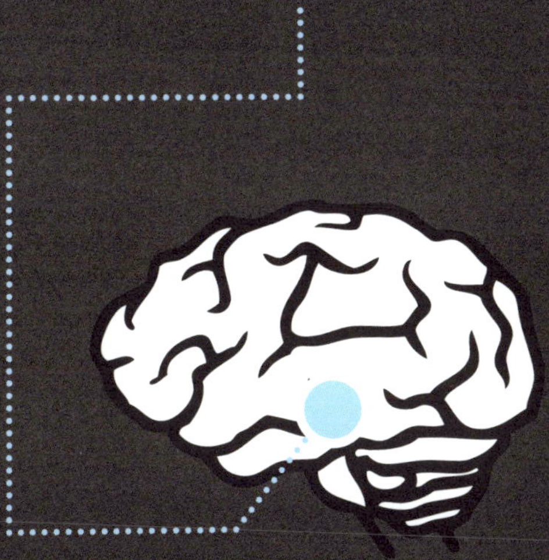

The left **TEMPORAL LOBE** is important for processing speech and vision. It is responsible for comprehension, but also emotional association and retaining visual memories.

“WHAT YOU WEAR IS HOW YOU PRESENT YOURSELF TO THE WORLD, ESPECIALLY TODAY WHEN HUMAN CONTACTS GO SO FAST. FASHION IS INSTANT LANGUAGE.

**MIUCCIA PRADA,**
**FASHION DESIGNER**

**Language is essential to every interaction** and situation in our business lives. It is vital to us all because we use it to communicate with the people around us what we feel, what we value, what we desire and need and question/understand. We communicate with our words, along with gestures and tone of voice, in a multitude of situations. And we will alter our style of communication according to emotions and context – for example, you wouldn't speak in the same way to someone who likes you to be direct as you would to someone more sensitive. Being able to communicate with flexibility helps us to form positive relationships, create understanding, connect and promote teamwork. Successful Business Brains appreciate that communication drives our inner self and allows us to better ourselves.

# PERSONAL BRANDING

Why is developing an identity that resonates with people so important? Personal branding is about being clear about who you are and communicating what separates you from the norm. It's about being unique and relevant, so that you can achieve your business goals and become sought after. All Business Brains know that if you understand your own talents, strengths, skills, passions and values, you can use this information to really stand out. A strong, authentic personal brand helps you to become known for what you're good at, what sets you apart from everyone else and can position you as an expert.

Know what is important to you. Know what quality looks like. Invest in understanding the sort of expectations people will have of someone like you and surpass them. Enjoy being passionate about trends in technology, fashion, culture, politics and design. All of these areas have something to add to the world around you and can help you to engage with others, so ignore them at your peril. And remember that looking the part is also part of the brand process: stand out as if you mean business.

A powerful personal brand will help you to:

- project your ideas and values to others because they know who you are and what you stand for
- sell your product or service because knowing who you are creates confidence
- sustain resilience in times of difficulty because you're unique – 'niche', if you like – and therefore valuable
- become competitive because you will be clear and distinctive
- stimulate a presence that means something to you and others who believe in something similar.

Now think about your mission and what your personal brand stands for. Consider the following:

4.1a

**IMAGE: who do you need to look like?**

Are you more David Beckham than Wayne Rooney? Lady Gaga than Liza Minnelli? Bill Gates than Mark Zuckerberg? Karen Brady than Anita Roddick? Be clear about their look. Cut out images. See them clearly and form a 'look' that resonates with yourself and your mission.

**4.1b** **ROLE MODELLING: who do you need to think like?**

This is not about impersonating someone else, but about being influenced by those you admire. Research the people you have in mind – their story, their values and beliefs. Read quotes from them. Explore their mindset.

**4.1c** **CULTURE: be on the edge of your brand.**

What is going to change over the next year or two? Where is the world headed and how can you move with it? What books can you read?

Business Brains know who they will need to impress and what sort of impact they need to make.

LADY GAGA got dropped by a major record label after only three months. As of 2015, she's sold about 23 million albums worldwide and is a brand in her own right.

# ELEMENTARY, MY DEAR WATSON

Sherlock Holmes was famous for his incredible use of questions. He was a master of language and knew exactly how to frame a question to create clarity and unambiguous thinking. Business Brains also appreciate that sensitive use of language will help to open up their thinking and understanding of other people's perceptions of reality.

Consider using questions within frames, to keep the conversation from straying. Here are some examples, but you can create your own frames appropriate to the conversation.

### Perceptions

- How am I viewing everything?
- How does this view support me?
- How else could I view the situation?

### Judgement

- What is my overall judgement on this?
- How have I judged someone or something and is it helping?
- How else could I judge this person or situation?

### Feelings

- How do I truly feel about the situation?
- How do others feel?
- How does it affect my actions?
- How do I need to feel instead?

### Beliefs

- What do I believe is possible?
- What is important about this?
- What do I believe I am good at and how can this help me?

### Actions

- What can I do to help the situation?
- What can I do to take the first step?
- What actions would someone take who already knows the answer?

### Negative

| |
|---|
| What would be the most likely thing I could do to make it worse? |
| What steps do I need to take towards failing? |
| How could I fail to be successful on this? |
| Why do I think like this and what could I change to have more supportive thoughts? |

### Consequences

| |
|---|
| What will the consequences be to me and everyone concerned? |
| How willing am I to take the actions required and to deal with the consequences? |
| How could I minimise risk and maximise opportunity? |

**Try and design some of your own questions within each frame to get in the swing.** 4.2

**Now create a new frame called 'influence'. Design some questions and see what happens.**
Explore them. Answer them. Grow them.

## GET IN THE DRIVER'S SEAT

Getting clear on your internal dialogue helps you gain focus. Clearly defining your mission creates action, but before you drive on, you have to ask yourself:

What has made you choose this mission? Why is it so important to you?

To be truly motivated to achieve success you really need to know what has generated your passion in the first place. Only then can you truly understand why you need to follow this path. The answers to these questions are your purposeful values, and they are the intrinsic drivers that push your decision-making buttons.

Continuing to generate the thrust required to maintain focus and effort when faced with your old foes – complacency, apathy, challenge and fear – is the next trial. These deadly adversaries can appear at any time and shake your momentum. However, when you know your purpose you create a laser-like focus which keeps you on track regardless of what barriers and obstacles are thrown in your way.

**Purposeful drivers are:**

| | |
|---|---|
| To make a difference | To generate a change in society |
| To provide security | To be the best in the business |
| To create something unique | To be known as an expert in the field |
| To become wealthy | To be happy and satisfied |
| To enjoy freedom of choice | To help others less fortunate |

**What's the driver for your mission?**

4.3

**So to discover your purpose you must ask yourself the following 'importance' questions:**

What is important to me about achieving this outcome?

What will it give me?

Why is it of value?

What would happen if I didn't achieve it?

How will I know when I have achieved it?

Note: perhaps look at what you don't want instead as this may be a more powerful route for you.

## ANIMAL INSTINCT

When you think either of someone you admire or someone who may irritate you, then you will probably see that they act in certain ways. These 'ways' are specific behavioural patterns that define them in your head. As we know, we get on with some people more than others because of certain factors: it may be what they believe in, what motivates them, their passions, their hobbies and perhaps how they see the world and behave as a result. 'People like people like them' is a common phrase in rapport. Behaviour patterns are fascinating because, as a Business Brain, understanding these patterns will help you with self-awareness and building relationships.

As we explore some examples of these behaviour patterns you need to be aware of some rules:

- Exhibiting a particular set of patterns in a specific situation does not imply that you will follow the same pattern in everything, everywhere and at all times. Your preferences may change over time as you learn new information or experience significant events in your life.

- As you read the description of a pattern, if you have difficulty believing someone can think and behave in this way or if you struggle to relate to someone who lives their life like that, then you are probably at the other end of the spectrum. On the other hand, if you really connect to one of the patterns, then, this is mostly likely true for you. Of course, you could also be in the middle, between the two extremes.

- Being at one end of a pattern or in the middle is not necessarily better than being at the other. It's more about evaluating if this pattern is actually helping you or not. If it's not, then simply acting in a slightly different way that is more in keeping with the other end of the behavioural pattern may allow you to see and experience different outcomes and responses and therefore generate an increase in agility. This is always of benefit.

- You can identify a person's preferences from the language they use and/or their behaviours. If they exhibit characteristics from both extremes, then they are in the middle.

Think of the patterns as a line with two ends and a centre:

Remember: neither end is good or bad, but you must consider that your behaviours may alter based on the following elements:

**Context:** the scenario you are in may have a strong influence on your behaviour because it may engender different levels of response. When selling, for example, you may be really focused and diligent when planning a pitch, but when following up and closing the deal you may be more laid back, to the point where you sometimes lose out due to a lack of drive. Or you may be more alert in the morning compared to the evening when you like to relax.

**States:** certain emotional states might cause you to react in different ways. For example, being relaxed may help you to create new ideas and express yourself; however, it may not help you when making tough decisions.

Not many people are at the extreme ends of the pattern, but it does happen and you'll probably have met a few of them! Find your place on the scale, but remember that where you are on the pattern is often expressed in different ways and to different degrees at different times.

## PAIN OR GAIN?

There are times when we are inspired by our dreams and have a strong desire to 'move towards' our goals. On other occasions we feel more driven to avoid or 'move away from' a difficult situation or event.

When you're 'towards'-driven you will tend to see all the good in something – the benefits, if you like. You will be motivated by your goals. You may well be thinking in positive terms and therefore use positive language such as 'want', 'take risks', 'achieve', 'gain', 'seek', 'attain' and 'look forward'. Towards-based thinkers will either know what they want or have a good idea about it, and go about doing what is necessary to get it.

On the other hand, if you are more of an 'away-from' thinker, you are likely to use language such as 'don't want', 'avoid risks', 'resolve', 'minimise', 'crises', 'issues', and 'problems'. You will be on the lookout for perceived threats or challenges and you will be particularly aware of pitfalls and might have a tendency for seeking solutions.

Again – neither pattern is good or bad. There is room for both and each can be effective in its own way. Just make sure your pattern is working for you in any given situation.

For example, if you are in need of critical thinking because you are facing a perceived threat to your business, being fully 'towards' could be irresponsible. In such a scenario a more 'away-from' style of thinking and behaving would potentially make you more resourceful. If, on the other hand, you are looking at attaining a qualification which may enhance your chances of success, then being more 'towards' may support you because your self-talk would potentially lead you in the direction of a more focused, outcome-led mindset.

When selling an idea, service or product you should notice this pattern and influence accordingly.

**Where and when do you behave more as a toward or a away from person?**

4.4

Context 1: When investing in something

← towards | away →

Context 2: When taking risks

← towards | away →

Now consider some situations of your own where you are more of a toward person and some where you focus more on an away from approach – what initiates the shift?

# GETTING CHUNKY

We all like information to be given to us in a scale that makes us feel comfortable: too much and it can become intimidating; too little and we can become worried that we are under-informed. This is often referred to in terms of 'chunk size'. So 'big-chunk' thinkers like top-level information or an overview first, they talk in generalities and can be a little overwhelmed by too much detail. When developing a goal they will start by taking an holistic helicopter view and simply start with the goal in mind. 'Small-chunk' thinkers, on the other hand, are more comfortable with the detail. They enjoy exploring all elements first and putting the puzzle together, and don't like being spoken to in vague terms that lack substance.

Big-chunk language includes generalisations such as:

Everyone can do it. | Nobody believes this idea. | It's impossible.

Small-chunk language tends to use phrases such as:

The smaller elements include … | What parts make up the overall idea?

Let's get down to the specifics. | Tell me about what exactly needs to happen next.

You can chunk down by asking questions such as:

How did you dothat? | Why did that happen? | What happened about …?

What, specifically …? | Tell me more about … | What is the root cause of all this?

Or you can chunk up by asking questions such as:

What does this mean? | How does that relate to …?

Let's look at the bigger picture … | What are we trying to achieve here?

Who is this for? What do they really want?

Armed with this ability, you can:

- create ideas and support brainstorming.
- write proposals that work for the reader.
- communicate accurately to your staff and clients.
- plan and organise your time and projects effectively.
- coach and communicate with people in a targeted fashion.

One great way to appreciate chunking is to use it to solve problems. Try to:

- start at a high level of chunking to really define the initial problem.
- chunk down to find possible challenging elements.
- chunk up to review and agree the overall value in resolving the challenge.
- chunk down to build an understanding of the problem.
- chunk up to look for problems in the overall system.
- chunk down to find specific actions to address.

**Where and when do you behave more as a big chunk or a small chunk person?**

**4.5**

Context 1: When writing a proposal

Context 2: When problem solving

Now consider some situations of your own where you are more of a big chunk person and some where you move more towards small chunk – what initiates the shift?

## A JOB WELL DONE

How do you know when you have done a good job? Do you say to yourself, 'I think it's gone well' or, 'It felt good, so I'm confident that it was well received' or, 'I don't know how I know – I just do'. Or maybe you are thinking in terms of 'When I receive the feedback' or, 'The results generated are most important' or, 'When I see them enjoying themselves'?

If you relate to the first style of thinking, then you take more notice of your internal voice and feelings; if, on the other hand, the second style resonates with you, then you enjoy receiving feedback from outside sources such as other people's opinions, reading books and doing research.

An understanding of this pattern is critical when delivering feedback. An internally referenced person is more likely to refrain from seeking others' opinions and can become rather defensive. An externally referenced person must have feedback in order to evaluate their own progress; if you ask a strongly external individual how they think they are doing they will probably respond, 'How do *you* think I'm doing?'

**Where and when do you behave more as an internal or external person?**

**4.6**

Context 1: When giving a presentation or chairing a meeting

← internal voice    external feedback →

Context 2: When designing a brand or product

← internal voice    external feedback →

Now consider some other situations where you are more of an internal person and some where you become more external – what initiates the shift?

In certain situations what would happen if you were to move slightly more towards the opposing pattern? What might change? If you are internally referenced, what would it mean to be open to receiving feedback? Or, if you are externally referenced, what might happen if you simply used your own beliefs, values and judgment to come to a conclusion?

# I THINK I FEEL SOMETHING

Association is a term used to refer to getting fully 'into' an experience: when you see what you see, hear what you hear and feel what you feel. Actors like Robert De Niro and Christian Bale, for example, are exceptionally talented at understanding how to embrace a role fully and live in the shoes of the person in question.

Disassociation is the opposite: thinking more as an outsider, stepping out of the 'self' and looking from the outside in. This technique is useful for taking balanced perspectives, meditation, pain management and behaving effectively in certain kinds of challenging situations.

When a person runs a fully associated pattern they often get 'stuck' which can be unpleasant, painful, inappropriate, confusing or in some other way negative. This can be really tough if you are trying to achieve success because you may reassociate into tricky situations that didn't work in the past and therefore shy away from doing them. Public speaking is a classic example where many people struggle with this idea.

On the other hand, a disassociation pattern can create an inability to use empathy and to connect in relationships and, as such, it can be a serious business problem – especially in networking, leadership and selling. A lack of warmth and not connecting with people and/or situations may generate the feeling that your intentions are not solid and people may, as a result, refrain from working with you.

**Where and when do you behave more as an associated or a disassociated person?**

**4.7**

Context 1: When under stress or pressure

← association disassociation →

Context 2: When managing conflict

← association disassociation →

Now consider some situations of your own where you are more of an associated person and some where you move more towards disassociation – what initiates the shift?

# SAME DIFFERENCE

Do you notice what is the same or what is different about something?

When a person notices commonality – likenesses and similarities – they are a matcher. When they notice differences – dislikes and contrasts – then they are more of a mismatcher.

Matching is important for rapport and relationship-building because it shows we 'like' someone's ideas or attitudes. It expresses agreement and therefore similarity. Sameness can bring people together. Overly matching can become problematic at times, however, because you can lose sight of your own needs, values and uniqueness of 'self'. Being compliant all the time is good for neither party.

Mismatching is essential to some people because it helps when sorting out concepts and thoughts. If you can't tell any difference between two or more things, they are basically identical and you have no basis on which to evaluate them. 'Defining the difference helps me to understand something.' Overly mismatching, however, can become challenging for many people as they may see you as being disagreeable or lacking empathy.

**4.8** **Where and when do you behave more as a mismatcher or matcher?**

Context 1: When being pitched to

← mismatcher matcher →

Context 2: When being taught something new

← mismatcher matcher →

Now consider some situations of your own where you are more of a mismatcher and some where you are more of a matcher – what initiates the shift?

BRAIN BOOSTER FIVE:

# INFLUENCE

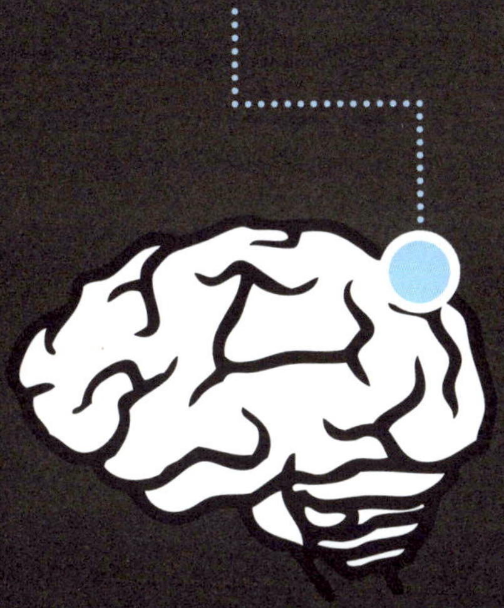

The **PARIETAL LOBE** processes sensory information and helps understanding of the world around you. Several portions of the parietal lobe are important in language processing.

“THINK TWICE BEFORE YOU SPEAK, BECAUSE YOUR WORDS AND INFLUENCE WILL PLANT THE SEED OF EITHER SUCCESS OR FAILURE IN THE MIND OF ANOTHER.

**NAPOLEON HILL,**
**AMERICAN AUTHOR**

**You've generated a fantastic business idea** or designed an essential new product. Perhaps you're just ambitious and want to make a difference in your life. Either way, you now need the ability to convince everyone to support you, your dreams and your vision. The problem is that not everyone believes what you believe. Not everyone is seeing the world as you do.

Influencing others is a challenging concept for many people, which is why it's worth understanding some of the psychological principles behind the influencing process. It's also just as important to appreciate the rules of influence within yourself and to hone the requisite inner tools to make the necessary changes to become a successful Business Brain.

In this chapter, we'll examine these principles, and look at how you can apply them to positively persuading and influencing others (as opposed to manipulating or enforcing decisions).

# WHAT DO YOU REPRESENT?

All our experiences are a result of what we see, feel, hear, smell and touch – indeed, how our senses convert information. In rapport terms, we call these senses our representational systems, and we need to understand how people view the outside world to help us to influence their responses.

Here is some simple information to help you grow your rapport skills.

### Visual People

Behavioural clues: they like images, colours and shapes; they are head-up people, who stand upright; their voice is high-pitched, they speak fast and breathe high in the chest. In addition they may:

- be more interested in how a product looks than how it feels
- be flamboyant in appearance
- notice a lot about you.

To influence them you should consider the following:

- Use pictures to explain your point.
- Be visually creative with the environment.
- Be energetic.

Words used: 'look', 'focus', 'imagine', 'see', 'watch', 'colour', 'dim', 'notice', 'perspective'

Phrases used: 'I see what you mean', 'something to look forward to',
'future looks bright'

## Auditory People

**Behavioural clues:** they love words; their head is tilted to listen; their voice is melodic; they breathe mid-chest. In addition:

- they love reading
- they often talk to themselves
- they enjoy expressing themselves by telling rather than showing.

To influence them you should consider the following:

- When possible, give them something to read, as well as telling them.
- Ensure you use the right words and tone.
- Be clear and unambiguous.

**Words used:** 'say', 'loud', 'sound', 'remark', 'silence', 'listens'

**Phrases used:** 'on the same wavelength', 'speak from the heart', 'I hear what you say'

## Kinaesthetic People

**Behavioural clues:** they enjoy emotional connections; they are head-down and often use a lower, softer voice. In addition:

- they can be emotional about events that you may not care about
- they feel experiences
- they can be spontaneous.

To influence them you should consider the following:

- Use empathy.
- If possible, be tactile.
- Use gestures and be animated.

**Words used:** 'touch', 'warm', 'cold', 'solid', 'hold', 'heavy', 'gentle', 'soothing', 'weak', 'hot'

**Phrases used:** 'get to grips', 'cool customer', 'heat of the moment'

## Auditory-digital People

**Behavioural clues:** they are often internal thinkers, so give little away; they are not very action-orientated as they like to reflect first. In addition:

- they keep track of all their experiences
- they categorise their experiences
- they like to plan and set directions.

To influence them you should consider the following:

- Use your communication skills to summarise events and views clearly.
- Make sure you comment on data and facts.
- Always draw conclusions.

**Words used:** Create, process, system, think, understand, experience, data

**Phrases used:** 'we need to access', 'understanding the system', 'I think it may be this'

Words are the most obvious clue to help you decide which sensory preference people generally like to use. As an example, what do you notice about the following four sentences?

**You have shown me a bright idea on how to proceed and I would like to look into it further.**

**You have told me of a way to proceed that sounds good and I would like to hear more about it.**

**You have handed me a way to proceed that is on solid ground and I would like to get more of a feel for it.**

**You have provided me with a way to proceed that makes sense and I would like to have more details.**

The first sentence uses visual words, the second auditory, the third kinaesthetic and the fourth auditory-digital – yet all four sentences convey the same general meaning.

Look at the list below and consider some more sensory words that you might need to be aware of:

| Visual | Auditory | Kinaesthetic | Auditory-digital |
|---|---|---|---|
| see | hear | feel | sense |
| look | listen | touch | experience |
| view | sounds | grasp | understand |
| appear | make music | get hold of | think |
| show | resounding | slip through | learn |
| dawn | tune in/out | catch on | process |
| reveal | be all ears | tap into | decide |
| envision | ring bells | connect with | motivate |
| illuminate | silence | throw out | consider |
| imagine | be heard | turn around | change |
| foggy | deaf | unfeeling | insensitive |
| focused | mellifluous | concrete | distinct |
| hazy | dissonance | scrape | conceive |
| picture | unhearing | solid | inform |
| dim | remark | cling | incorporate |
| clarify | pronounce | numb | interpret |
| inspect | enquire | gaze | acquire |

5.1a **Get in some practise by thinking about more sensory-based words and phrases that you may use or hear. List your words/phrases here:**

| Visual: | Auditory: | Kinaesthetic: | Auditory-digital: |
|---|---|---|---|

5.1b **For two minutes, describe your ideal holiday using only visual words.**
**Then, for the next two minutes use only auditory words, for the next two minutes use only kinaesthetic words and for the final two minutes use only auditory-digital words.**

5.1c **Listen to the predicates that your business contacts, friends or family members use.** They will use a mixture of visual, auditory, kinaesthetic and auditory-digital predicates, but one or two will be used more frequently and this is their preferred representational system.

# CHANGING MINDS

Change can be a big influencer. Some people love exploring new stuff, while others are influenced by keeping things stable. But all great Business Brains embrace risks and seek out positive change. Yet for many of us, change is exceptionally difficult – even when we know it makes sense.

## The ten components of change

Change expert Stan Goldberg, Ph.D. has identified the ten principles that he believes are necessary for successful self-change. They are really simple but often we can overcomplicate 'stuff' to make change more difficult, or even impossible. We can push away control and responsibility, so that what we want is somehow never within our reach. We might tell ourselves stories, such as:

**I am powerless**

Ironically the belief that you are helpless and not in control of situations is incredibly powerful. 'I can't do anything about my situation' is a powerful barrier to facilitating change.

**I am a victim of circumstance**

If you believe this, then it helps support a lack of action. It means that fate has played a part in everything you want and you can't actually make anything happen – even though it is painful to remain where you are.

**I pretend**

Being in denial is damaging because even though you don't truly believe your own thoughts, you uphold them to protect yourself. This allows you to share excuses with others and means that you are creating a poor reality. People who have pretended that things have changed are likely to say, 'I can't believe it happened again ...' when the perceived new outlook fails and the old, self-defeating situation replays itself again.

So let's take a look now at the ten rules for change:

1. **Break down the behaviour into parts**
   Most behaviours can be broken down. Separate your desired behaviour into smaller, self-contained parts. Take fear of the unknown as an example. This may be built around three components. Firstly, you may worry about failing before you even start. Secondly, you may have experienced failure before when attempting something new, so you actually worry about not being good enough. And thirdly, you may be so concerned about what else might happen that you haven't considered if you push on with the change. Now, meet each of these head on and reframe your thoughts on them.

2. **Change needn't be scary**
   Because change is a journey we often don't fully know what we are going to get. But why not think about consequences in constructive ways? For example, the idea of trying to lose weight may seem daunting, but imagine if you succeed – what else may then come your way? More energy? More self-confidence? Greater ability to make better choices and meet new people?

   At the same time, don't create unrealistic missions and goals: make them tough, but not so tough that you start to fear them.

3. **Make change positive**
   Change shouldn't be painful. It should have resourceful, constructive and bright connections. Imagine 'carrot'-based rewards for achieving the changes you want. In fact, why not reward yourself every time you meet deadlines, achieve milestones or even the outcome itself?

4. **Being is actually a lot easier than becoming**
   Too often we will make the process of change painful and undesirable. One of the great elements of change is embracing the fact that the process should be one of continuous learning and improvement. Take it easy and stop applying unnecessary pressure to yourself. Measure your gradual achievements and enjoy each one as you become the change itself.

5. **Be more mindful**
   Life is far too cluttered. We rush through it expecting and not creating. Become more aware of your change and everything about it that's important. Take your time to plan the change. Measure it out like a timeline and experience everything with conscious awareness.

### 6. Because you are aware, it reduces surprises

Being aware is always a powerful place to be. It helps us to know where we are now and where we want to be. It can also support who we need to be to get there. Don't be afraid of feedback. Seek it out and learn to manage the experience with passion. Assess all parts of the change. Be fond of becoming a solution as you progress.

### 7. Structure and change work together

If you are a spontaneous/creative type of person, then being organised can sometimes be undesirable, but this is a limiting attitude when it comes to change. Being structured in your approach is a vital cog in the mechanics of change. It gives you focus and attention to the core parts. Make a list of everything within the change model you desire. Give everything a place in time and resources. Write it down and get going.

### 8. Practise, practise, practise

If you want to change something then you must practise what it takes to make this change permanent. Never forget this basic but most important principle, otherwise the change may take longer to effect and become more challenging. Change isn't always easy – you need to work at it. But it is rewarding. Even better, find someone who has been there and get their support.

### 9. Protect your change

Ensure you maintain your new behaviour or mindset by protecting it through constant reassessment. Look at your environment and ensure it helps support the change. Make sure you surround yourself with the right people and find all the resources you need to sustain the change.

### 10. Chunk down the small outcomes

When you do this each step becomes a separate mission and you'll eventually arrive at the end goal. Just creating and working through a series of mini goals can help you feel motivated and can drive positive achievement.

**5.2** **Now, consider something you want or need to change and apply the above ten principles.**
What did you find?

## THAT'S LOGICAL, CAPTAIN

*Star Trek*'s Mr Spock was very logical. He loved being factual and put aside emotion at almost every opportunity. This is great in theory – however, if only he had known about the Logical Levels model his life would have been a whole lot easier.

Inspired by anthropologist Gregory Bateson and developed by the pioneers of neuro-linguistic programming (NLP), the Logical Levels model is very helpful in designing any action plan for influencing change in either yourself or others, and does so by:

- helping you gain clarity on how you/they experience a situation
- underlining the specific level at which you need to influence change
- highlighting challenges in relationships and helping you to find targeted solutions.

Imagine someone who plays an important part in your business life needs to be influenced to see things differently to generate a positive change. Take a look at the table below and see how the levels can work in terms of targeted intention.

| | |
|---|---|
| **Mission/purpose** | What would be the positive purpose of the change for them? |
| **Identity** | Who are they and what needs to change?<br>How do they need to see themselves? |
| **Beliefs/values** | Why is this going to be important to them? |
| **Capability** | How can we make this change happen? |
| **Behaviour** | What do they need to do to change? |
| **Environment** | Where do they need to change? |

Next, let's say you have created a new invention that you think is great for someone's business. You may experience them rejecting it through one or more level:

| | |
|---|---|
| **Mission:** | " I don't see the purpose of it. |
| **Identity:** | " I don't see how it can benefit me. |
| **Beliefs/values:** | " I don't see the value in it. |
| **Capability:** | " I don't know how it can help my business. |
| **Behaviour:** | " I can't see how we can implement it into our business. |
| **Environment:** | " I can't see us using it here. |

The key here is to influence them by tackling the specific level of communication they are targeting. This may well open up the conversation more easily and get to the root issues more effectively, which by the way, may well sit at a different level, as we know.

5.3 **You can even use logical levels to kick-start your business idea. Fill in the levels below and see what you find. It may help influence your next steps.**

**Mission:** what is the point of this business to me and/or others?

**Identity:** who would I need to be to make this a success, who is my target market?

**Beliefs/values:** what are my company values and why/what value does my business add to others?

**Capability:** how can I make this business a success, what processes do I need and how can I sell what I do to potential buyers?

**Behaviour:** what can I do to inspire staff, sell to clients and serve customers and what do my customers want to experience from my business and its product?

**Environment:** where do I need to be located, when do I launch and where is my target market?

# WHICH HATS DO YOU WEAR?

Business Brains are good at influencing people. They appreciate differences in personality, plus other people's quirks and can, therefore, affect the flow of communication and motivation successfully. This can then shape the relationship itself.

Personality is an interesting topic. It is thought that fifty percent of your personality is genetically determined and is, as such, rather tricky to change. The remaining fifty percent comprises two differing traits: character and attitude.

Character is created from elements such as:

- your parents – their beliefs, values, preferences and quirks
- your cultural and social circles
- your peers and what they consider to be normal and acceptable
- humour, risk and love perspectives.

Your attitude, however, is intrinsically based and therefore harder to influence. Your emotional management and attitude are, arguably, ingrained.

There are many personality models to pick from. However this simple HATS assessment is very easy to use and as you probably have now guessed, is a huge generalisation. It says that around seven to eight billion people on this planet will fit into four 'types':

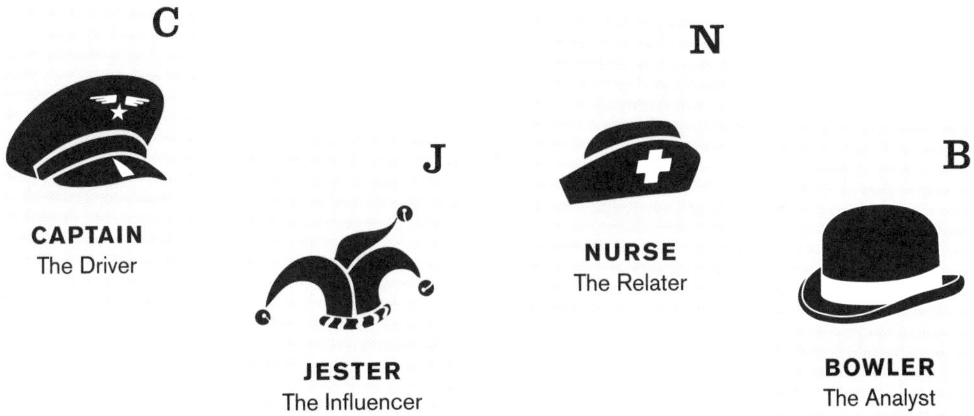


We use 'hats' because a) jobs and pastimes can often reflect people's character and b) they are flexible – you can take them off and swap them around which gives you agility. Obviously context, status, relationships, etc. will all also have an impact on behaviour, however it is useful as a model. Why – I hear you ask again? Well, because you make a judgement on someone within the first seven to 30 seconds of meeting them – a generalisation based on your personal experience. You then chunk down deeper into the 'relationship' to establish a more profound understanding of that person the more you get to know them. HATS can help you to observe simple patterns of behaviour in certain situations that can support your perceptions and rapport levels and therefore enhance communication and influence.

The following exercise will allow you to understand the HATS in more detail and add context to the equation, therefore helping you to add power to your communication.

You embody all the hats at some level, but taking a particular situation or relationship, ask your friends and family how they see you within that context. Ask them to read the hat profiles and consider how would they evaluate you in those terms – which would be your primary hat, secondary, etc.? Be open to their views; do not try to reject them as this is their personal view, their experience. Explore and understand:

- How did they come to this conclusion?
- Which hat do they think you potentially need more of to get better results in the same situation?
- What do they see as your strengths and weaknesses?
- If you swapped your primary hat for your lowest-level hat, what do they think might change for the better?

It is really vital to gain the views of others because this expands our mental-mapped experiences and gives us greater awareness of ourselves.

Next, pick someone you know and do the same for them in the context of your relationship. Consider the following:

- What is their hat order and why do you think this?
- What does their hat order need to be so that your relationship can improve?
- What elements of each hat can you influence to improve the relationship?

With each hat profile I have also given you the opportunity to connect some of your clients or colleagues to each hat and note down the evidence to support this view.

C

## CAPTAIN

**General characteristics:** direct · decisive · high ego strength · problem-solver · risk-taker · self-starter · IQ

**Value to team:** bottom-line organiser · places value on time · challenges the status quo · innovative

**Possible weaknesses:** oversteps authority · argumentative attitude · dislikes routine · attempts too much at once

**Greatest fear:** being taken advantage of

**Motivated by:** new challenges · power and authority to take risks and make decisions · freedom from routine and mundane tasks · changing environments in which to work and play

**Ideal environment:** innovative focus on the future · non-routine challenging tasks and activities · projects that produce tangible results · freedom from controls, supervision and details · personal evaluation based on results, not methods

**Remember – high-C personalities may want:** authority · varied activities · prestige · freedom · assignments promoting growth · 'bottom-line' approach · opportunity for advancement

✓ **DO:** be brief, direct and to the point · ask 'What?' not 'How?' questions' · focus on business – remember they desire results · suggest ways for them to achieve results, be in charge and solve problems · highlight logical benefits of featured ideas and approaches

× **DON'T:** ramble or repeat yourself · focus on problems · be too sociable · make generalisations · make statements without support

CAPTAIN:

**While analysing information, a high-C may:** ignore potential risks · not weigh the pros and cons · not consider others' opinions · offer innovative and progressive systems and ideas

**Positive characteristics in teams:** autocratic managers – great in a crisis · self-reliant · innovative in getting results · maintains focus on goals · specific and direct · overcomes obstacles · provides direction and leadership · pushes group towards decisions · willing to speak out · generally optimistic · welcomes challenges without fear · accepts risks · sees the big picture · can handle multiple projects · functions well with heavy workloads

**Personal growth areas for C behavioural styles:** strive to be an 'active' listener · be attentive to other team members' ideas until everyone reaches a consensus · be less controlling and domineering · develop a greater appreciation for the opinions, feelings and desires of others · put more energy into personal relationships · show support for other team members · take time to explain the 'whys' of their statements and proposals · be friendlier and more approachable

5.4 **List three clients or colleagues who display a HIGH CAPTAIN personality.**
Also list your evidence.

J

## JESTER

**General characteristics:** enthusiastic · trusting · optimistic · persuasive · talkative · impulsive · emotional · EQ

**Value to team:** creative problem-solver · great encourager · motivates others to achieve · positive sense of humour · negotiates conflicts · peacemaker

**Possible weaknesses:** more concerned with popularity than tangible results · inattentive to detail · overuses gestures and facial expressions · tends to listen only when it's convenient

**Greatest fear:** rejection

**Motivated by:** flattery, praise, popularity and acceptance · a friendly environment · freedom from too many rules and regulations · other people being available to handle details

**Ideal environment:** practical procedures · few conflicts and arguments · freedom from controls and details · a forum to express ideas · group activities in professional and social settings

**Remember – high-J personalities may want:** social esteem and acceptance · freedom from details and control · people to talk to · positive working conditions · recognition of abilities · opportunity to motivate and influence others

✓ **DO:** build a favourable, friendly environment · give opportunity for them to be vocal about ideas, people and their intuition · assist them in developing ways to transfer talk into action · share testimonials from others relating to proposed ideas · allow time for stimulating, sociable activities · submit details in writing, but don't dwell on them · develop a participative relationship · create incentives for following through on tasks

× **DON'T:** eliminate social time · do all the talking · ignore their ideas or accomplishments · tell them what to do

**JESTER:**

**While analysing information a high-J may:** lose concentration · miss important facts and details · interrupt · be creative in problem-solving

**Positive characteristics in teams:** instinctive communicators · participative managers – influence and inspire · motivate the team · spontaneous and agreeable · respond well to the unexpected · create an atmosphere of wellbeing · enthusiastic · provide direction and leadership · express ideas well · work well with other people · make good spokespeople · will offer opinions · persuasive · have a positive attitude · accomplish goals through people · good sense of humour · accepting of others · strong in brainstorming sessions

**Personal growth areas for J behavioural styles:** weigh the pros and cons before making a decision · be less impulsive · be more results-orientated · exercise control over their actions, words and emotions · focus more on details and facts · remember to slow down for other team members · talk less · listen more · consider and evaluate ideas from other team members · concentrate on following through with tasks

5.5 **List three clients or colleagues who display a HIGH JESTER personality.**
Also list your evidence.

# N

## NURSE

**General characteristics:** stable · reliable · good listener · team player · possessive · steady · predictable · understanding · friendly · EQ

**Value to team:** reliable and dependable · loyal team worker · compliant towards authority · good listener · patient and empathetic · good at reconciling conflicts

**Possible weaknesses:** resistant to change and takes a long time to adjust to it · bears grudges · sensitive to criticism · has difficulty establishing priorities

**Greatest fear:** loss of security

**Motivated by:** recognition for loyalty and dependability · safety and security · no sudden changes in procedure or lifestyle · activities that can be started and finished

**Ideal environment:** practical procedures and systems · stability and predictability · tasks that can be completed at one time · few conflicts and arguments · a team atmosphere

**Remember – high-N personalities may want:** security in situations · sincere appreciation · repeated work patterns · time to adjust to change · limited territory of responsibility

✓ **DO:** create a favourable environment – personal and agreeable · express genuine interest in them as a person · provide them with clarification for tasks and answers to 'How?' questions · be patient in drawing out their goals · present ideas or departures from current practices in a non-threatening manner · give them time to adjust · clearly define goals, procedures and their role in the overall plan · assure them of personal follow-up support · explain how their actions will minimise the risks involved and enhance current procedures

× **DON'T:** be pushy, overly aggressive or demanding · be too confrontational

NURSE:

**While analysing information, a high-N may:** be openly agreeable, but inwardly unyielding · internalise their concerns and doubts · hesitate to share feedback during a presentation · slow down the action · provide valuable support for team goals

**Positive characteristics in teams:** instinctive relaters · participative managers – accomplish goals through personal relationships · make others feel like they belong · show sincerity · can see an easier way of doing things · focused and intuitive about people and relationships · full of common sense · buy into team goals · dependable · identify strongly with the team · strive to build relationships · provide stability · consider elements of a project as a whole · realistic and practical · even-tempered · provide specialised skills · show patience with others · loyal

**Personal growth areas for N behavioural styles:** be more open to change · be more direct in interactions · focus on overall goals of the team, rather than specific procedures · deal with confrontation constructively · develop more flexibility · increase pace to accomplish goals · show more initiative · work at expressing thoughts, opinions and feelings

**5.6** **List three clients or colleagues who display a HIGH NURSE personality.**
Also list your evidence.

B

## BOWLER

**General characteristics:** clear · accurate · analytical · conscientious · careful · fact-finder · precise · high standards · systematic · IQ

**Value to team:** 'the anchor of reality' · conscientious and even-tempered · thorough in all activities · defines situation · gathers, criticises and tests information

**Possible weaknesses:** needs clear-cut boundaries for actions/relationships · bound by procedures and methods · gets bogged down in details · prefers not to verbalise feelings · will give in rather that argue

**Greatest fear:** criticism

**Motivated by:** standards of high quality · limited social interaction · detailed tasks · logical organisation of information

**Ideal environment:** tasks and projects that can be followed through to completion · specialised or technical tasks · practical work procedures and routines · few conflicts and arguments · instructions and reassurance that they are doing what is expected of them

**Remember – high-B personalities may want:** autonomy and independence · controlled work environment · reassurance · precise expectations and goals · exact job descriptions · planned change

✓ **DO:** prepare your case in advance · delineate pros and cons of proposed ideas · support ideas and statements with accurate data · reassure them that no surprises will occur · submit an exact job description with a precise explanation of how the task fits into the big picture · review recommendations with them in a systematic and comprehensive manner · be specific when agreeing · disagree with the facts rather than the person · be patient

× **DON'T:** refuse to explain details · answer questions vaguely or casually

## BOWLER

**While analysing information, a high-B may:** become overly cautious and conservative · get too bogged down in details · avoid or postpone decisions, especially if they perceive a risk · be an effective troubleshooter

**Positive characteristics in teams:** instinctive organisers · 'do-it-yourself' managers – they create and maintain systems · strive for a logical, consistent environment · control the details · conscientious · evaluate the team's progress · ask important questions · maintain focus on tasks · offer conservative approaches · emphasise quality · think logically · will share risks and responsibilities · work systematically · will strive for consensus · diplomatic · will analyse obstacles

**Personal Growth Areas for B Behavioural Styles:** concentrate on doing the right things, not just doing things right · be less critical of others' ideas and methods · respond more quickly to accomplish team goals · strive to build relationships with other team members · be more decisive · focus less on facts and more on people · take risks along with other team members

5.7 **List three clients or colleagues who display a HIGH BOWLER personality.**
Also list your evidence.

BRAIN BOOSTER SIX:

# THINKING

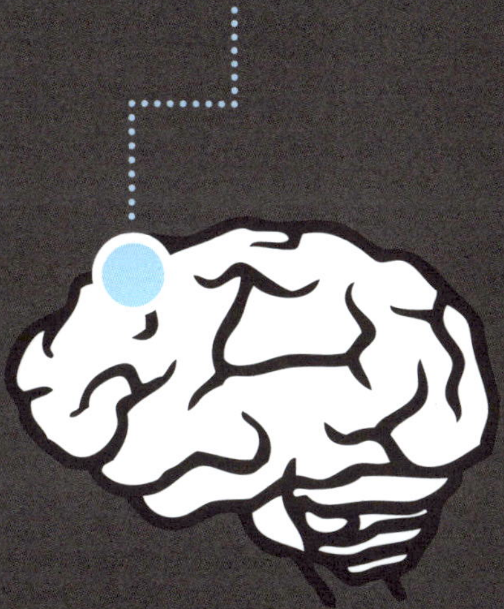

The **FRONTAL LOBE** is responsible for planning, problem solving and decision-making. The basic activity of this brain region is considered to be orchestration of thoughts and actions in accordance with internal goals.

“YOUR TIME IS LIMITED, SO DON’T WASTE IT LIVING SOMEONE ELSE’S LIFE. DON’T BE TRAPPED BY DOGMA – WHICH IS LIVING WITH THE RESULTS OF OTHER PEOPLE’S THINKING. DON’T LET THE NOISE OF OTHERS’ OPINIONS DROWN OUT YOUR OWN INNER VOICE. AND MOST IMPORTANT, HAVE THE COURAGE TO FOLLOW YOUR HEART AND INTUITION.

**STEVE JOBS,**
**CO-FOUNDER, CHAIRMAN AND CEO OF APPLE**

**Business Brains appreciate that thinking comes in differing forms.** Strategic thinking will support you by helping you to achieve your goals more rapidly – so success comes as a result of thinking about how you can proactively accomplish your outcomes, instead of just reacting to situations and conditions. A strategic mindset also encourages you to determine the best use of resources at your disposal and how to align them with your desired aims. Creative thinking can help you become more agile in how you respond to people, ideas and problems. It can encourage curiosity and generate progress. Analytical thinking can provide you with a way of exploring details and ensuring that you don't miss anything.

The ability to think in various ways can only help to make you become more resourceful as an individual and a successful Business Brain.

# MASTERY

To become a Business Brain you must get to the point where you're a master in your field. You have to be passionate about it and that means having an emotional connection to it. Because it's made up from various parts mastery can include boring elements that are essential to becoming an expert, and this is why being in love with what you do is critical to your success.

How do you work out what you want to master? First, you need to explore; don't hang around and wait for it to happen. Try different things. Get involved in lots of interesting 'stuff'. It's very rare for someone to just wake up and know what they are destined to do, so get out there and enjoy the experience of finding out. Once you've decided, then focus and become dedicated to being an expert. This is where the magic happens and where you hit the famous 10,000 hours of dedication that truly make you a master in your field. It's the self-generated process of immersing yourself into your craft where you focus on learning above all else, and gain the fundamental skills of mastery.

### What are the challenges to mastery?

**Distraction** The world is constantly evolving and not always in helpful ways. The power of social media and more accessible communication means that you can be in danger of losing focus – the biggest challenge to mastery.

**Lack of persistence** Know what your mission is and constantly keep motivated towards the outcome. The journey to mastery should be fulfilling in its own right, but knowing the overall purpose is key to being a master.

**Self-doubt** Keep your self-talk positive and resourceful – even in times of difficulty (which will happen, believe me). The route to mastery is not easy. If it were, everyone would excel. Hold yourself together and appreciate the small steps of achievement.

**Now, what do you want or need to master in order to achieve you mission?**
How can you get started and where can you go to find the answers to your art?

6.1

BILL GATES didn't appear to be destined for greatness after dropping out of Harvard and starting a first business with Microsoft co-founder Paul Allen – Traf-O-Data, which subsequently failed. But while this early idea didn't work, Gates' later work did, creating the global empire that is Microsoft.

# LEARN HOW TO GROW

Business Brains understand that success doesn't always come easily. You have to embrace challenges and overcome barriers.

One proven approach that helps with problem-based thinking and supporting the development of any mission is the GROW model. GROW, in this context, is an acronym standing for:

| | |
|---|---|
| G | **Goal:** establish where you need/want to be |
| R | **Reality:** where you are now |
| O | **Options/opportunities:** the choices you can create to get to where you want |
| W | **Will:** how motivated are you to make this happen? |

The model is a simple yet powerful framework for structuring any coaching or mentoring session. However, Business Brains often use this technique for developing their thinking and problem-solving abilities. A useful metaphor for the GROW model is the plan you might make for an important journey. You start with the map which helps you to decide where you are going (the Goal) and establish where you currently are (the current Reality). Then you explore various ways (the Options) for making the journey. In the final step, establishing the Will, you ensure you're committed to making the journey and are prepared for the conditions and obstacles you may meet along the way.

**Step 1** **Establish where you need/want to be**

Identify a personal challenge, limitation or problem you want to improve on. Make overcoming it a mini challenge in your overall mission.

First, you must define the problem and then the desired outcome to be achieved. Useful questions include:

6.2a **What exactly are you looking to achieve instead?**
**How will you experience it?**
**How will you know that you have solved the problem and achieved the desired goal?**
**How will you know the problem is being resolved as you progress?**

## Step 2 Examine current reality

Next, ask yourself to describe your current reality. This is a very important step: too often, people try to solve a problem without fully considering their starting point, and often they are missing some of the information they need to solve the problem effectively.

Useful questions include:

**6.2b**

**What is happening now and how is it a problem?**
**Is the problem built around a person, product or experience? If so, can you clearly define it?**
**What is the effect or result of the problem?**
**Where are you now compared to where you need to be?**

**Step 3** **Explore the options**

Once you have explored the current reality, it's time to look at what is possible – all the options you have for solving the problem. Generate as many good ones as possible.

Useful questions include:

6.2c **What else could you do to resolve the challenges you face?**
**What if the constraints were removed – what choices would you create to resolve the problem?**
**What are the benefits and downsides of each option?**
**What factors must you use to weigh up the options?**

**Step 4** **Establish the will**

By examining your current reality and exploring the options, you will now have a good idea of how you can find potential solutions and achieve the desired goal. That's great – but in itself, this may not be enough! So your final step is to encourage yourself to commit to specific action. In so doing, you will help yourself establish your own will and motivation.

**So what will you do now and when should it happen?**
**What could stop you moving forward?**
**And how will you overcome it?**
**Will this address your goal?**
**How likely is this option to succeed?**

6.2d

Today Disney rakes in billions from merchandise, movies and theme parks around the world, but WALT DISNEY himself had a rough start. He was fired by a newspaper editor because 'he lacked imagination and had no good ideas'. After that, Disney started a number of businesses that didn't last long and ended with bankruptcy and failure. However he kept focus and self-belief and eventually found a recipe for success.

# YOUR DISNEY STRATEGY

When you have big ideas they can be rather intimidating. And then self-sabotage can occur. We tend to push away what we truly want because it can sometimes be easier to deal with failure by not actually moving in the desired direction. This can be for a number of reasons:

- We've been programmed as kids not to dream and to just 'get a job'.
- We have had great hopes at certain stages in life, but they came to nothing.
- We've failed in the past and decided that's how life is.
- Positive thinking from self-help gurus hasn't worked either.

So how can you help yourself to become more resourceful in your thinking? Todd Epstein and Robert Dilts devised a technique to address just this, based on their discovery that when Walt Disney had a plan for a new film he appeared to use three frames of thinking: dreamer, realist and critic.

## The three vital roles

The Disney Creativity Strategy separates out three vital roles – dreamer, realist and critic – involved in the process of generating creative ideas and translating them into reality:

**Dreamer** This is the brainstorming role. Ask yourself, 'What do I really want?' Do not let reality come into your thoughts – consider instead what, in an ideal world, would your mission become? Who would you become?

**Realist** This is the 'put-your-plan-into-action' role. What would need to happen to make it real? How could you do it? Think constructively. Devise an action plan and evaluate it to determine what is realistic. Ask yourself, 'What will I do to make these plans a reality?' Establish time frames and milestones for progress. Make sure your plan can be initiated and maintained by the appropriate person or group.

**Critic** This is the problem-solving role. Think of all the difficulties and unwanted consequences. Evaluate them. Ask yourself, 'What could go wrong?' Think about what is missing, what is surplus, what the consequences will be.

**Using a business idea or challenge you have, take it through the three zones.** 6.3

Don't get confused. Explore each of the three zones in detail and spend at least twenty minutes in each.

Dreamer zone:

Critic zone:

Realist zone:

When you've completed this, ask yourself: what has changed and what actions will you take?

**The wacky author of brilliant books such as *The Grinch* and *The Cat in the Hat*, DR SEUSS was actually originally rejected by twenty-seven different publishers before his first book *And To Think That I Saw It On Mulberry Street* was first published.**

# INNOVATE, MATE!

If you're an aspiring Business Brain with a new idea, product or process then try the SCAMPER technique. It is attributed to Bob Eberle, author of books about creativity for children aimed at teachers. **SCAMPER** is a mnemonic model for seven thinking techniques that can help you to come up with unique solutions to problems – and it's incredibly simple in its approach. The seven techniques are as follows:

**S** **Substitute** processes/people/product

Think about substituting a part or parts for something else. By looking for something to substitute you can often stimulate new ideas.

**C** **Combine** with other functions/teams/people

Think about combining two or more parts to achieve a different product/process or perhaps to enhance a particular element of something.

**A** **Adapt** functions/skills/awareness

Think about which parts of the idea/product/process could be adapted to change their value/importance/meaning.

**M** **Modify** brand/product/service

Think about altering a part or all of the current idea/product/process, or perhaps distort it in an unusual way. By doing this you can often generate positive alternatives.

**P** **Put to other use** new versions, combined uses

Think about how to put your current idea/product/process to other uses or think of what you could reuse from somewhere else in order to solve problems.

**E** **Eliminate** inefficiencies/reduce/simplify/ineffectiveness

Think about what might happen if you eliminated parts of the idea/product/process. It may reduce time, simplify processes and improve effectiveness.

**R** **Reverse** viewpoints/processes/uses

What if part of it worked in reverse or was done in a different order. What would you do if you had to take action in reverse?

**Now, let's look at some of the questions that could be asked for each of the seven thinking techniques and then why not create some of your own?**

S **Substitute**

What elements can you substitute to improve the idea/product/process?
What other types of products or processes could you use to improve things?
If you were to substitute certain process what might happen?
What will happen if you substituted your values towards the idea/product/process?

C **Combine**

What would happen if you combined someone else's idea with your own?
How would combining other people's viewpoints with yours enhance everything?
What would happen if you joined forces with the competition?
If you combined your abilities and talents with someone else's what might happen?

A **Adapt**

What else is the idea/product/process like?
Who or what could you role-model to enhance the idea/product/process?
If you changed the context, where else would it work well?
What other idea/product/process could you use for inspiration?

M **Modify**

If you changed your outlook to become more cynical/positive/creative what would happen to the idea/product/process?
How could you change the look and feel of your idea/product/process?
What elements could you bring to life to help create more value?
How could you modify an element to enhance the idea/product/process?

**Put to other use**

P

If the idea/product/process was to be used in a different situation, where might it work?
In what other industry can people use your idea/product/process?
How else could you make the same things happen by doing something else?
What elements could you recycle to make something new?

**Eliminate**

E

What elements/restrictions could you eliminate to make the idea/product/process more successful?
What parts could you remove to make things easier?
How could you make the idea/product/process cheaper, easier, faster, more effective or affordable?
If you eliminated something to make life easier what would it be?

**Reverse**

R

What would happen if you reversed everything?
What would the impact be if you do the opposite of what you're doing now?
What components could you substitute without compromising on the core value?
What could you definitely not afford to reverse or swap?

**6.4** **Now, take some of these questions and explore the answers below. Then think about what ideas and solutions you've generated and make those alterations. Review your findings.**

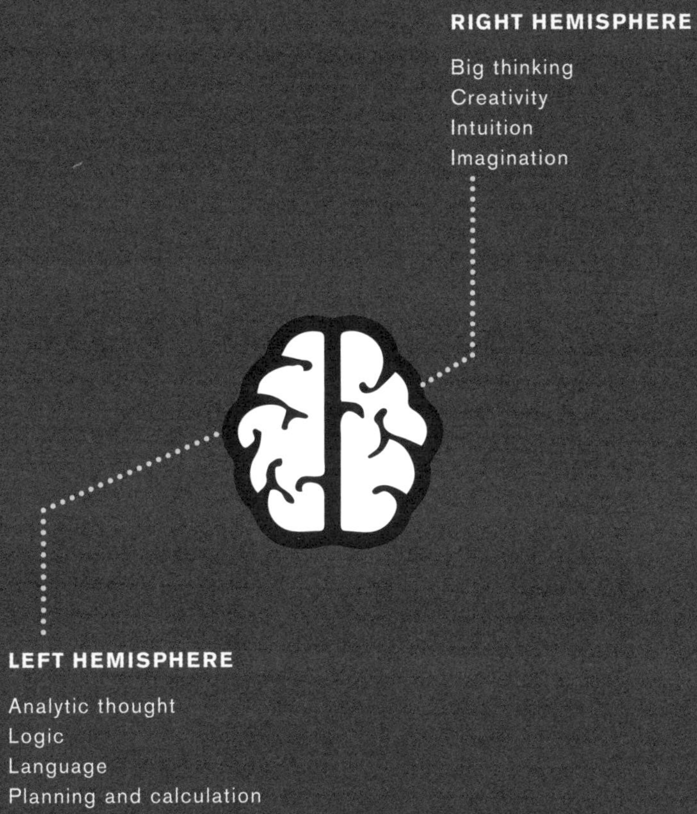
RIGHT HEMISPHERE
Big thinking
Creativity
Intuition
Imagination
LEFT HEMISPHERE
Analytic thought
Logic
Language
Planning and calculation

# CHECKLIST:

**Did you do all your workouts?**
**Tick off the exercises you completed.**

| | |
|---|---|
| What it is that you want to achieve? | ☐ |

## BRAIN BOOSTER ONE: MINDSET

| | | |
|---|---|---|
| 1.1 a,b,c | Mission possible | ✓ |
| 1.2 | Being Steven Spielberg | ☐ |
| 1.3 | Your Super Self | ☐ |
| 1.4 a,b,c | Super-Self-Talk | ☐ |
| 1.5 | Role model | ☐ |
| 1.6 a,b,c | Falling is good | ☐ |
| 1.7 a,b | Choosing choice | ☐ |

## BRAIN BOOSTER TWO: RELATIONSHIPS

| | | |
|---|---|---|
| 2.1 a,b,c | Heart and head | ☐ |
| 2.2 | EQ: the six domains | ☐ |
| 2.3 | What's your positive intention? | ☐ |
| 2.4 | Excuses drive you nowhere | ☐ |
| 2.5 a,b,c | Why do you exist, folks? | ☐ |
| 2.6 | Your Network = Your Net Worth | ☐ |

## BRAIN BOOSTER THREE: PERCEPTION

| | |
|---|---|
| 3.1 | If what you're doing isn't working, do something different |
| 3.2 | The art of framing |
| 3.3 | You've been framed |
| 3.4 | Life through a lens |
| 3.5 | Landscaping your brain |
| 3.6 a,b | Changing the landscape |

## BRAIN BOOSTER FOUR: LANGUAGE

| | |
|---|---|
| 4.1 a,b,c | Personal branding |
| 4.2 | Elementary, my dear Watson |
| 4.3 | Get in the driver's seat |
| 4.4 | Pain or gain? |
| 4.5 | Getting chunky |
| 4.6 | A job well done |
| 4.7 | I think I feel something |
| 4.8 | Same difference |

## BRAIN BOOSTER FIVE: INFLUENCE

| | |
|---|---|
| 5.1 a,b,c | What do you represent? |
| 5.2 | Changing minds |
| 5.3 | That's logical, Captain |
| 5.4 | Which hats do you wear? - Captain |
| 5.5 | - Jester |
| 5.6 | - Nurse |
| 5.7 | - Bowler |

## BRAIN BOOSTER SIX: THINKING

| | |
|---|---|
| 6.1 | Mastery |
| 6.2 a,b,c,d | Learn how to GROW |
| 6.3 | Your Disney Strategy |
| 6.4 | Innovate, mate! |

| **Trait/Quality/Aptitude** | **Score** (1-10) | **Why is it important?** What will it give me? | **How can I generate it?** Who do I know who possesses it and what can I do to tap into this? | **How and where can I use it?** What is the 1st step for implementation? |
|---|---|---|---|---|
| 1. | | | | |
| 2. | | | | |
| 3. | | | | |
| 4. | | | | |
| 5. | | | | |

## FINAL WORKOUT
# MAPPING EXCELLENCE

One of the key activities in generating success is using people who are recognised as excelling in their respective fields as role models. What is it about them that makes the difference in their performance? When these differences have been identified they can be communicated to other people who can then learn to perform with a similar level of skill. Having said that, the person who is learning must have the necessary aptitude and be willing to carry out the necessary self-development. In other words, while it is easy enough in principle to use as a model the activity of a world class sprinter, for example, a person who has a physical limitation, is severely overweight or who refuses to commit to the dedicated effort of practise, is unlikely to be able to translate the modelled information into a personal skill.

In the exercise opposite simply list six traits, qualities or aptitudes that would allow you to become brilliant at your role, then score your current competency in these areas from 1 to 10 (1 being the lowest level and 10 being the highest – and thus the ultimate aim). Next, complete the question sections to support your thinking and help you re-evaluate these qualities as part of your new mapped approach.

MUHAMMAD ALI was born Cassius Marcellus Clay Jr. on January 17, 1942 in Louisville, Kentucky. Ali became a Golden Gloves champion and Olympic gold medallist within two years of each other. Ali won all of his competitive bouts in the 1960s, the majority of them by knockout. Even whilst fighting Parkinson's disease in his retirement, Ali has devoted much of his time to philanthropy. In 2005, Ali received the Presidential Medal of Freedom from President George W. Bush. He also opened the Muhammad Ali Centre in his hometown of Louisville that same year. 'I am an ordinary man who worked hard to develop the talent I was given,' he said. 'I believed in myself and I believe in the goodness of others,' said Ali. 'Many fans wanted to build a museum to acknowledge my achievements. I wanted more than a building to house my memorabilia. I wanted a place that would inspire people to be the best that they could be at whatever they chose to do, and to encourage them to be respectful of one another.'

Ali is arguably, the self-proclaimed *greatest* athlete of all time.

## EVALUATE YOUR WORKOUT

It is always important to evaluate your activities and results, digesting and reflecting on how you have performed in and embraced the areas of development. Use these questions to help support your new learning.

**What results have you discovered?**

**What challenges did you face?**

**What have you learned from the exercise?**

**How has possessing your new traits improved YOU?**

## AUTHOR'S DEDICATION

This book is dedicated to all the people who have had such a powerful impact on my life. My amazing friends, associates and relationships that have shaped my past, present and future and of course my family. Mum – my empathy and support. Dad – my creativity and drive. Simon and his family – my inspiration and playfulness. Lydia – my supporter and balance. And of course Sara, who in her absence will never truly know the full impact her wonderful presence had in my life.


## PUBLISHER'S ACKNOWLEDGEMENTS

I want to thank Oliver for trusting me with the creation of his book. It was a joy to work with him. Although I have spent many weeks with the book now, at the time of going to print, I still haven't found the time to do the workouts myself, but cannot wait to make some time and reap the benefits of the Business Brain programme myself.

We are indebted to Anne Newman for going through the drafts so meticulously and not being afraid to challenge us. Thanks to Charity Green for proofreading and looking at the book with a fresh eye.

John Bond and Tim Inman for their good advice.

The many friends and colleagues who saw the book at various stages and helped to make it better with their feedback and comments.

## ONLINE RESOURCES

You can find out more about the Business Brain programme and get additional resources and videos online:

www.oliverthompsontraining.co.uk

www.the-business-brain.com

The Business Brain on Youtube:
bit.ly/business-brain-youtube
(shortened link)

Facebook:
www.facebook.com/ottraining

#businessbrain